Led By Fire
An Incredible Story

Charles & Betty McGee

PRESS

Led By Fire
An Incredible Story
by Charles & Betty McGee

Printed in the United States of America

ISBN 9781613791844

Some of the names of people and places have been changed to protect the innocent.

www.xulonpress.com

DEDICATION

W e want to dedicate our book to our Parents, Nellie & George McGee and Hazel & William Berry. Without their tender love and care we would not be where we are today. We're so grateful for their prayers, encouragement, and direction in our lives.

We also want to dedicate this book to our son, Charles Barry McGee and our daughter Christina Marie McGee. Their encouragement and input made this book possible.

And last, our granddaughter, Sharon Connie Briel who is always so eager to hear our story.

ACKNOWLEDGEMENTS

Thank you Robert Limbaugh and Dave and Laura Knorr for the many hours you spent with us doing re-writes of our original manuscript.

Thank you Pastor Ken Gaub for your prayers and your idea for our book cover and your assistance in getting our book to different publishers.

We want to thank Pastor At and Nyretta Boshoff for their many years of friendship. Thank you for your love and encouragement; and for your willingness to write the forward to our book.

Thank you Krista Krieg for all your work on the cover design; and thank you Jeff Furman for taking our picture for the cover.

We want to say a very special thank you to Pastor Ron and Connie Coleman for their faithful prayers; their friendship and encouragement; and most of all, for their love. Without their love and support, our book might not have gotten this far.

Thank you all so very much and bless you!

FORWARD

R eading through the pages of this book brought back so many wonderful memories that we had as the Boshoff family with the McGee's. Our very first trip to their home in Morija, Lesotho (Southern Africa) left one with a tangible feeling of God's presence and an incredible warmth. We felt at home with them from the very beginning. Betty's home made pies were always a firm favorite.

This story begins with turmoil in Maseru, Lesotho when the boarders were closed and many homes were burned to the ground as shooting was rampant for almost a week. Their story is one of love, tears, struggles and triumphs that will speak to the very soul of the reader. They share a rare passion for life and for the Kingdom of God that is contagious to anyone they come into contact with. This passion emanates from the pages of their book.

We witnessed, first hand, some of their tears as Betty and Charles, together with their children, Barry and Tina, were faced with racial prejudice and how they managed to overcome every hurt and go through life with a bounce in their step and a glint in their eyes.

Your faith will be challenged and strengthened as you read this book and see how they share the "real" moments of exhaustion and fear and cry out to God and see His hand in it all.

Pastors At and Nyretta Boshoff
Christian Revival Church – 35,000 members
Bloemfontein, Orange Free State
Republic of South Africa

INTRODUCTION

C harles and I have often talked about the way the Lord has constantly had His hand upon us in a very real way. We are very grateful for the way He has led us, guided us, protected us and shown us His mercy and grace in every area of our lives.

We used to talk about the way He brought us together and how He helped us get married. We wanted to try to write about it, if for no other reason, so that our children would see the strong hand of God in our lives.

Because of some of these discussions, I sat down and tried for several years to write a book about some of our experiences. I just could not do it. I got bogged down with it every time and would leave it for years. Then I would try again, re-write the bit I had started and give up again, all too soon. It just would not flow and was too much of a struggle.

Then on New Year's Eve in the year 2000, I felt God speaking to my heart. I felt He was saying, "Write what I've done in your life, as I give you the idea's." I shared this with Charles and he was very excited about it.

Sure enough, the next morning, New Years Day, 2001, right after my quiet time with the Lord, I remembered an event and wrote down a few notes. Later that day, I typed the event and it went smoothly. Then I felt God saying, "Don't struggle, just let it flow, as I give you the idea's." I was busy praising God and I felt Him again, speaking to me. "Your book will be finished before the end of the year." I was more excited.

Charles and I shared with our son and daughter what we felt God was saying and they too were very excited about it and encouraged us to 'go for it!'

It has been fun and easy to work on this book together. It is the prayer of our hearts that God would speak to your spirit as you read this book. We are so grateful to God for His constant presence and His constant protection in our lives. He has taught us so much about trusting Him and knowing that His Word is our truth to stand on.

We pray that you too, will learn that God is your source in every area and He is the only one we can completely depend upon in every situation.

Ephes. 3:20 Now unto Him that is able to do exceeding abundantly above all that we ask or think according to the power that worketh in us.

Chapter 1

THE VOTE

Explosions flickered on the television screen as the international news reporter spent sixty seconds on the "political unrest" in LeSotho. As I reached for the phone for the umpteenth time that day, I fought anxiety. I knew I shouldn't be afraid, but fear tried to hold my heart in its grip. The American consulate had warned us before I left and now; I had seen the destruction on the news myself. The small African country surrounded by South Africa had caught the world's attention. I cried, "Charles! Where are you? Did you get out before they burned Maseru?"

My thoughts spiraled. Was this really to be the end? After all we'd been through, would I really lose Charles when we were 7,000 miles apart? NO! Surely not! My mind refused to accept that possibility. We had been through far too much together. My thoughts flew back to when I first knew Charles.

I'll never forget that night when my Father walked into our home and said, "Betty, there's a business meeting at the church tonight. We're all going to that meeting. We need every member to vote."

I thought it a little odd that he would ask me to do something like this. I was only 13 years old. I asked, "What's going on? Why do I need to be there to vote?"

"You'll find out when we get there."

When we arrived, I could see that this was not an ordinary meeting. As I walked in I could overhear conversations about "this colored boy" and "does he even want to come to church here?" A lot of other kids my age were there.

I sat down next to my friend, Judy. "Hey, what's going on here? My dad just told me to come, but he didn't say what it was about."

She turned to me. "You don't know?"

I shook my head, "no."

"Well, it seems Lloyd was at Frey's getting his car fixed and he witnessed to this colored man. And the man got saved."

"Good for him." I said.

Judy went on, "Problem is, though, there's no colored churches in town."

"What do you mean, 'no colored churches,' why can't he come here?"

"That's what this is all about. We've never had any colored people come to our church before. We need to decide if we want to let them come."

I was incredulous. "How can we decide who to let come into this church and who not to?"

The pastor stood up and said, "Let's open with a word of prayer."

My mind went into overdrive. Even though I had my own feelings and beliefs, I knew that this would not be an easy problem to resolve. For me, it was clear that people were people. My parents taught me that. When I was younger, my best friend, Carla, was African-American. Racist sentiments were foreign to me. However, we lived in Chester, a small town in Southern Illinois.

This was 1954. The town was mostly white, with a few black families. The movie house, the only restaurant, the swimming pool, and most of the churches were for whites only. To its credit, the schools were desegregated years before it had become the law of the land. However, change took time, and the town still remained pretty much a segregated community. The white people in town never really considered themselves "prejudiced." They just didn't really associate with anyone who was "colored".

Rev. Sloan began, "I'm turning the meeting over to Lloyd."

Lloyd began, "Well, there's not much to it. I've been talking to Charlie McGee at Frey's about church and salvation. It really bothered me that they have no place to go to church. Anyway, the more I talked to him, the more curious he got and he got saved."

At that there were approving sounds from the crowd. It's always good news when someone gets saved.

Lloyd continued, "You know, now that I witnessed to him and he's born again, he's got no place to go to church. You know, that's just not right. I thought that, well, maybe he could start to come to church here. I mean, can't we open our church doors to Negroes?"

The next sounds were not so approving. There were murmurs from the crowd, and I could feel the tension begin to mount.

The first voice in the crowd countered. "If we do, then would we have to open our doors to everyone?"

Lloyd responded, "Would that be bad?"

Roy came back, "It is one thing to open our schools up to all races, but is it necessary to open up our churches?"

And, with that, the debate began. The longer it went on, the angrier people became.

Many voices started up.

"The Catholics have opened their doors to them. Why can't we?"

"Look, we want people to be born again. If riff raff come into our church, others may stay away."

"Hey! Wait a minute! We've all known the McGee family for a long time. Their family is well respected by almost everyone in the community!"

"I know that, but if we let them come in, then all the others can come in, too. We can't say that just the McGee's can come in."

Several nodded in assent.

"If we cannot love our brother whom we can see, how can we love God, whom we cannot see?"

"We just want what's best for our church."

"And what about our children?" a lady shouted.

"Suppose your daughter came home and said she had a date with a Negro?"

"We're not talking about dating; we're talking about going to church together."

"They have a church in Sparta. Why can't they go there?"

"Why should they drive all the way to Sparta? We're supposed to love one another." Sparta was a little over twenty miles away.

"They will know we are Christians by our love."

"What about our children? We need to protect our children."

I was really horrified. People were getting angry and yelling at one another. What were they so afraid of? I just did not understand this at all.

The battle went on....

"We need to teach them, too, don't we, to love others?"

"We're just asking for trouble by letting them into our church."

"What kind of trouble?"

"...All kinds of trouble; just think about it! There must be boundaries!"

By this time, Lloyd was as angry as the rest. "You're getting way ahead of yourself. We can talk to our kids. We're talking about worshipping God together with our brother Charlie McGee!"

"That's just the beginning of the trouble. There will be many more coming. When they see the McGee's coming to this church, there will be others coming. You wait and see!"

"And what's wrong with that?"

"What's right with that? That can lead to all kinds of trouble. Yes, we know the McGee's. But some of these others, we know about them and much of what we know we do not like."

"Are we here to make a difference; to reach out to a dying world; to save the lost? Or are we just a holy huddle that doesn't care about others?"

"We can care about others and reach out to the lost without mixing with these Negroes."

"Don't we care if the Negroes get saved?"

"Of course we care about them, but is it our responsibility to get them saved?"

"It's our responsibility to share Jesus with those we meet every day, no matter what race they are."

"You may feel that way, but I don't feel that way."

At that, I leaned over to Judy and whispered, "Are these people really believers?"

She whispered back, "It sure doesn't look like it!"

I didn't want to hear any more. I began to pray...

It was close to midnight when a frustrated Lloyd Peterson stood up and shouted, "Hey, everybody, we've talked long enough. It's time to vote now."

Reverend Sloan stood up. "OK, everyone, all in favor of opening the doors of our church to all races, raise your hand."

I looked around and saw that everyone my age had raised their hands. The pastor counted out loud: "…thirty-five, thirty-six, thirty-seven, …and thirty eight. OK, now, all those opposed?"

Again he counted out loud. The count came to thirty-five. By three votes, we approved that all races could be invited to our church. At that point, several left in a huff. I thought to myself, "How can this cause so much strife with so many people? How can believers act like this?"

That was the first time I had heard very much about Charles McGee

Chapter 2

GOSSIP

Gradually, Charles became an integral part of the church. He ushered. He taught Sunday school as well as "training union" on Sunday nights. And, he began to help with the youth in the Church.

I loved Charles' teaching because he walked the talk and; I trusted his counsel. One time, I had a real crush on a boy from our youth group so I dated him. But when we went out he became an absolute octopus. I went straight to Charles to talk with him about it. He said, "You just walk away from him." I took his advice.

I saw Charles as a mighty man of God, who believed in Jesus Christ as his Lord and Savior. He was a man, who seemed to know the Word of God and trusted God in every area. He always took time to really hear what people were saying. He was honest, he seemed to be a man of integrity and he cared about people. We all loved him.

The youth group, which had kids ranging in age from 14 to 24, enjoyed the activities Charles always planned for us. Sometimes it was skating, or basketball or hiking in the park. They were all fun things to do, and everybody who wanted to come was included. He even arranged for transportation.

There were New Year's parties and Halloween parties–all in a safe context. No one was ever injured–even with kids doing the driving.

In the summer of 1957, I had the opportunity to attend a Baptist summer camp on prayer. Each morning during my stay at this camp, we were taught from the Bible on how to listen and hear His voice for ourselves. In the afternoons we would go out into the woods and pray, writing down what we thought God was saying to us. During this time I remember two things specifically that I wrote down: 1.) I would be a missionary in Africa. 2.) God had a wonderful man that He would bring into my life; a pastor, who would serve in Africa with me.

When I returned home from camp that weekend, I couldn't wait to share my thoughts and prayers with my Sunday school teacher (Charles), who had helped me so much in my walk with the Lord.

I also had a chance to talk with our new pastor, Rev. Newton. He asked me if I would share my testimony with the congregation on the following Sunday. Being an enthusiastic teen, I was more than happy to do so. It never occurred to me that the ease of sharing my heart with Charles and the pastor wouldn't be the case with the whole congregation.

That Sunday, after the sermon, Rev. Newton invited me up to the pulpit. I looked out across the congregation and saw everyone staring at me. My tongue stuck to the roof of my mouth. I could not speak! Not a word! My mind raced. I was so scared I felt I would faint. Suddenly, I felt God's love coming from deep within me. It was so powerful. After what seemed a long time, I opened my mouth and a testimony of the goodness of God just flowed out of my mouth. After the service, the first person to tell me how well I did was Charles. I knew it was only God that helped me speak at all.

One Sunday afternoon in late spring, my aunt on my father's side fell and my parents took her to the hospital. I really wanted to go to church that night, so I decided to leave early and walk even though it was a couple of miles from my house to the church. About two-thirds of the way there, Charles drove by and spotted me. When he offered me a lift, I gladly accepted. I'd rather ride than walk any day.

Within minutes we were at the church. I hopped out of his car and walked up to my friends.

By the time the meeting was over, my parents were home. I called my Dad and he came to pick me up. On the way home, I told him how my teacher had given me a ride, and how nice he had been. He just nodded.

The very next morning, the phone rang. When I answered, the voice on the other end snarled, "Hey, Betty, if you're gonna screw around with that nigger, why don't you screw around with me?"

Then I heard the click as he hung up.

I just stood there, still holding the phone, staring at it. I couldn't fathom what I had just heard or the reason behind it.

At first I didn't say anything to anyone and no one asked. But only a few minutes later the phone rang again. It was another obscene phone call, very much like the last one. This time my mother saw my face. She looked over and asked, "What was that all about?"

I repeated what the caller said. Mom grabbed the phone and, of course, there was nobody there. She said, "Don't answer the phone again." Then she told my father and they told me not to answer the phone until the calls stopped.

I began to wonder. Did this have something to do with that ride to church, yesterday? Did someone actually think that there was something else going on? It hit me with fear; what would Charles think if he knew what was happening to me?

Within a week, we had become the talk of the town. The gossip had escalated to the point that I had even gotten pregnant and gone away to have an abortion.

A week later, I felt the tension in our home. Dad had gone out. Mom wore a worried look.

I spoke cautiously, "Mom, where's Dad?"

"I can't say right now, honey. When your father gets back, we'll know a little more."

I could tell things were not right and, somehow, I could just feel that the problem involved me.

Several hours later, the door opened and Dad walked in. He could see the concern on my face.

"Where were you, Dad?"

"Well, you know lots of people are upset about what they think is going on between you and Charles McGee."

My face flushed in embarrassment.

"Do you know what the Ku Klux Klan is?"

I nodded.

"It seems that there is some of that activity in town. They were talking about running Charles' family out of town and burning their house down."

"NO! I don't believe it." My first thought went to Charles and what was going on at his house right now.

My dad answered, "Nothing's going to happen. You don't need to worry about it."

My mind was screaming, 'Dear God, people want to run him out of town–him and his family!' It never even occurred to me that he too was being attacked–or even how people would attack him. He must be going through a lot worse than I've been going through! Has he been getting calls too? I need to talk to him. He probably hates me and wishes he'd never met me.

I ran to my mother. "Mom! I've got to call him!"

"No, Betty!" She quickly replied. "You can't do that!"

Dad interjected, "NO WAY! We've just spent hours trying to get things calmed down. We don't need a nosey operator reporting that you called him."

Then Mom said, "Betty, all you need to do is keep praying. Pray for Charles. God will protect him and his family. God is big enough."

I knew she was right. But I was scared—really scared, not for me but for him and his family.

Now, all these years later, I fought that terrible fear once again as I waited to hear from Charles. The solution hadn't changed either. I began to pray.

Chapter 3

MY FATHER

"What woke me?" Charles wondered as he glanced at the clock and saw that it was before dawn. "Were those helicopters?"

Here in Lesotho no aircraft flies at night. Instead of my normal morning prayer, I asked God, "What's happening?" Shortly after that, I heard large explosions, then automatic weapons fire. Bullets began to fly through the air all around the house.

I thought, "I promised Betty I'd be the first one out at any sign of trouble. But, it erupted so quickly. There's no way out now. If they catch me running, they would not hesitate to shoot. I'm trapped. God, will I ever see Betty again?"

I knelt in prayer and thanked God for his protection. I rejoiced to remember how faithful God had always been—even from the beginning of my relationship with Betty.

The trouble began when Rev. Newton called both Betty and me into his office.

The pastor spoke directly, "Charles, I'm sure you have heard the rumors going around town?"

"Yes, I have. I can assure you, Rev. Newton, that none of them are true. It all started when I offered Betty a ride to training union. I should have known better. I didn't think about something like this starting, but I should have. I am really sorry."

"So have you two been dating?"

Betty and I said simultaneously, "NO!"

"And you haven't been necking?"

"We have not been meeting or even holding hands." I was prepared to challenge anybody who said they'd seen something.

"So all of this talk is just malicious gossip," continued the pastor.

"That's *all* it is!" I answered resolutely.

The following Sunday, Rev. Newton spoke on gossip and what a terrible sin it is. After the service, several people approached each of us and apologized for what they had said and thought. I knew it was time for us to forgive and forget but it was not easy.

Frustrated, I knew what I had done and what I had not done. I am the kind of person who, if you saw me any place doing anything wrong, I wanted to be told about it. If people thought they'd seen something, I wanted to disprove it and to rebut their arguments. Here in our church, all that was swirling about was lies and no facts. It was very damaging to be lied about and those lies affected two people's lives — mine and Betty's.

I noticed a change in Betty and spoke to her after class one day. "Betty, I see a difference in you. You need to get before the Lord and let go of all the anger and bitterness. Guard your heart with all diligence. It will only hurt you more."

I knew that from my own experience. My father, George, had worked very hard to support our family. During the war years he had worked at a defense plant in St. Louis. After the war was over he secured a job as a prison guard in the Illinois State Penitentiary system, first at Joliet, then back in Chester at the Menard Correctional Center. Finally he had a pretty good paying job, and was at home on a regular basis.

Menard was one of three maximum-security facilities in Illinois, housing the most dangerous of criminals. It was a veritable fortress, built into the lower side of a bluff over-looking the Mississippi River. On one side there was the river, while on the other side a sheer cliff rose up to the top of the bluff. On top of the bluff was the "Security Hospital" which housed the criminally insane.

Just upriver from the facility were bottomlands with numerous bogs and sloughs. During the summer months mosquitoes would breed in the bogs upriver and migrate right down to the facility, attracted by the bright security lights. Sheltered by the bluff, the air was humid. It rarely moved. The summers were hot both for the inmates and the guards.

In the guard tower, where my father worked, the air was still as death. Mosquitoes flocked to the open area and became a nuisance. During this time, the prison provided the guards with an insecticide to combat the pests. Every night, he would spray his area and take his post in the guard tower. Because of the lack of airflow, the insecticide was usually effective for most of the night. Unfortunately, that exact condition also created a toxic environment for anyone working in the tower. Usually it was my father.

During the month of August of 1957, my dad became ill. He was off work for a week and grew increasingly ill with each passing day. By the end of the month he was admitted to a hospital in Redbud. His symptoms mimicked jaundice, but tests would not confirm it. As he grew weaker and weaker, he was unable to eat. Still, all tests were inconclusive.

It was a couple of weeks later that I was in church for Sunday night services. I sang in the choir. In the middle of the sermon, I saw my younger brother, Jim, in the back of the church. Jim was a massive man. But tonight his normally hulking frame was slouched. His face was tense. One of the elders from the church left his seat and went to Jim. The elder then came to the front of the church and gestured to me to join him. I slowly walked to the back of the church. Jim slipped his arm around me as we left the building. He told me that my dad was worsening and the doctors expected him to go at any time.

My brother, George, who had gotten leave from the United States Air Force, went with my mom back to the hospital. I had been there that afternoon.

I stopped by the Berry's house to let them know that my dad wasn't expected to last the night. He passed away at about 2 a.m. the next morning. When the doctors performed an autopsy on him, their report indicated an accumulation of insecticide in his body that eventually caused his death. My father had been poisoned.

Dr. Ringwald spoke with my mom afterward. He suggested that they get a can of insecticide from the prison so that they could recover damages from the state and at least cover funeral and medical expenses. However, by the time Jim got to the prison to recover a can, there were none to be found. No one knew anything about the insecticide. My mom decided not to pursue the issue. She knew it would just mean additional heartache and expense.

From that time on, Jim and I were the breadwinners of the family. My family scraped by on sharing, work, and pride. It was not easy, but we managed. We still had to pay dad's medical bills and I still had six younger brothers and sisters in school. Don was in college with a partial scholarship, and although he worked as well, we had to help him out, too. It was a difficult time for all of us. I asked God to help me and gradually I was able to forgive those who were too intimidated to speak on our behalf; and those who refused to pay any compensation to our family, and even those who were responsible for my Dad's death. Yes, it was hard but that was nothing new to me.

GOD'S MAN

My Mother told me I was born one cold snowy early morning in a small wood frame house with a little pot belly stove in the middle of the room. I was the second born into a family that later became a family of ten children. My parents were happy with their second son and all was well for over six months. Then suddenly, I would no longer take the breast milk, or any type of milk. When the Doctor agreed to take me off all milk apparently I was a happy baby again, but not for long. A few months later my Mother noticed something was amiss. I became sick, not sleeping and crying far too much and even running a fever that continued to grow higher. I was finally taken to the hospital where Doctors wondered if it could be appendix and decided to operate. They found their diagnosis to be correct but were surprised to find that I had a strangulated double hernia as well. The appendix burst before they were able to remove it and surgery was extensive. My life hung in the balance for weeks. After a very long recovery my Mom and Dad finally had their happy, healthy son back.

I grew up similar to most children my age, except that my world was smaller because I was not white. Life was tough in our home town with such a small minority group. Name calling was a regular offense and often my brothers and I were chased by small groups of youths who were looking for fun. We found ourselves dodging stones and often ran away to avoid street fights with some of the town bullies. My brothers, George and Jim were much more aggressive than I was and were quicker to defend them selves on a one to one basis. I chose not to fight unless I was really pushed into it. I chose to walk the path of peace wherever I could.

I had to go to work at a very early age to help pay the expenses because there was no health insurance and medical bills were extensive. My first jobs were cutting grass, weeding gardens and running errands for some of the white folk in town. I was usually paid fifteen or twenty cents per job. One time we got a job cutting an orchard with a push mower. My brother and I worked together all day in the hot sun on this orchard, cutting around the trees. The problem was that I could not work well in heat. I used to get very sick and started throwing up. Jim covered for me and tried to give me times to rest in the shade to cool down. We usually got one dollar each for this job. About mid afternoon, the owner of the orchard brought us a cool drink and a cocktail triangle sandwich and asked if we wanted it. We eagerly drank the drink and ate the sandwich, small as it was. We actually ate about four of them. They were not too fresh, but tasted good because we were really hungry. At the end of the day we were told, to our horror, that we would only get seventy five cents because twenty five cents was deducted for lunch. I later became a shoe shine boy at the barber shop and got more money in tips.

One special Christmas will always be remembered. It was the time that our Mom and Dad sat us down and said, "Children, Christmas is a special time to celebrate the birth of our Savior, Jesus Christ. Gifts are given because Jesus gave His life for us. We celebrate this season by giving gifts to one another. However, due to unexpected medical bills (Mom had Gallbladder surgery) we will not give gifts this year. We will praise God together for His goodness to us. Do not look for gifts, there will be none." My brothers and I talked about this a lot. We knew that Santa would remember us. We knew that we would get presents. Christmas morning came. We awoke early and eagerly ran into the living room. To our horror, there was no tree, no presents, and no smell of food cooking. We went back to play in our room, feeling disappointed and actually, feeling a bit of shock. Deep inside, we believed that somehow, something would be there for us, but we did not want our parents to see that we were disappointed. Later that day, there was a knock at the door. Mom opened the door and saw white folk standing at the door with boxes full of food and goodies. That happened two more times before the day was over. The next day, our family had a huge turkey dinner with all the trimmings. We all enjoyed our Christmas a day late!

I also remember another time when I ran into the kitchen with my brothers for supper and was told, "There is no food right now, we will eat later." We went to bed that night very hungry, having eaten nothing. The next day, there was still no food. No milk, no bread, no meal, no oil, no tea, no nothing. We went outside to play and forgot about our hunger for a little while. A neighbor lady called us and said, "Boys! Come here! I have something for you." We ran to her house and she gave us a large pot of cooked chicken and dumplings. We carefully carried it home and after praising God for His goodness we all feasted again. Our summer menu was mostly greens and fallen apples from an old overgrown, abandoned orchard. We loved fried apples and bread. My Father was able to get day old bread for five cents a loaf.

My first experience in church was attending with my family, a little AME church not far from where we lived. It was loud and lively, all black, with a powerful preacher. There were about five or six families attending. The church eventually closed because there were too few in the congregation. Most of the folks drove to a town about 20 miles away, but our family did not have a car. That was the end of church experience for me at that time.

I began my schooling at age five. I attended a small one room school which included grades one to eight years. There were about 8 to 15 students with one teacher. There was one boy in my class that used to pick out boys to beat up after school. He systematically challenged and attacked each new student. It finally came to the point that he came to me and said, "Charles, your day is coming. You're next on my list. I will choose the time and place. You're the only one I haven't whipped." Several days later the time had come. School was out and this boy approached me, laid down his jacket in front of me and said, "This is your day. Today, I'm going to give you a good whipping." With lightning speed, I hit him with all my might; three blows: two on the face and one in the stomach. He fell to the ground and I walked away. Within an hour, the boy's Father appeared at our home with the complaint that I had beat up his son with no reason. The Fathers began to talk about it. A little later, the other Father realized the truth and took his son home. That was the end of that boys fighting career in school. The teacher at this school had a boy friend and he often visited in the school-room while the students played outside. What I remember most about my school days is baseball and playing outside. I loved it. However, our parents were not too happy. They kept approaching the school board to do something about this school. They wanted a better education for their children.

In September, 1946, George and I were the first two blacks to integrate an all white High School in Southern Illinois. The school board had endorsed it, but some the teachers could not handle it. George refused to tolerate the abuse. He quit school after only two years and eventually went into the Air Force and completed his education and went on into Flight Aviation and later into the Nasa Space Program. I stayed but became very withdrawn and quiet. One teacher in particular used to use me as an example to the class. She often called upon me, knowing that I did not know the answer, and then explained to the class that this is why I did not belong in this school. She often pointed out the difference in the races and how one was far superior to the other. Yet another teacher saw in me the potential to learn and become an honor student. She took me aside and gave me special help and I began to do well and graduated with honors in June 1951.

During our junior year, the school took a class trip to a really nice country club and spent the day. We had only been at the club for about forty five minutes when a man came up to me and asked me to come into the office. After a lot of mumbling, they said, "There has been a big mistake. We did not realize that there was a colored man in this class. This club does not allow non whites. We have provided a car to escort you home. We will also pay you to leave quietly." The day was nearly half over when the students began to look for me. When they could not find me anywhere and went to the club management to further the search they were told that the policy of the club did not allow colored men in their club and they were not aware that Chester had colored students. The next day at school, the student body approached me and said that I had no right to make the decision on my own to leave without giving them all a chance to leave. It was then that I realized that they actually saw me as a fellow student and not as a black man. I really enjoyed my later years of schooling. My friends saw me for me.

Now, kneeling in prayer, my life was under attack again. I didn't know who the enemy was. They just rose up and tried to eat up those in authority. Once again, I prayed for relief, peace, and forgiveness.

Chapter 4

IN LOVE

The phone rang. It was Charles' brother. "Have you got the television on? Apparently, there's trouble there." Of course, I already knew that the whole of Maseru was in flames. He asked, "Have you heard from Charlie?" I had to answer no, but I believed in my heart that Charles couldn't be there. I refused to think of any other possibilities.

As I kept pushing scary thoughts out of my mind, thoughts of the past rose up within me

After dinner every evening, Ed, Bill, and I took turns washing the dishes. We were required to help out at a very early age. One particular evening, Ed was washing and Bill and I were drying. While my back was turned, Bill flipped me with a dishtowel. He made a good snap which left a red welt on my leg. I turned around and flipped at him. I wasn't too good at it, but the battle escalated. And then by accident, I got Bill a good one. He yelped and grabbed me, wrapping the towel around my neck pretending to choke me. Unfortunately he wrapped it a little too tight. Within seconds, everything went black.

It was so strange. Either the room started to spin, or I started to spin. I couldn't tell which. I felt as though I was beginning to descend – faster and faster. I was going down, down, down. The light at the top was growing dimmer and I found myself in total blackness. I was going down, feet first, still spinning. The light above me was now gone. It had faded away. I was in darkness – darkness blacker than anything I had ever seen. It was like I was being sucked down into a very deep pit. Was this hell? Was I dying?

The next thing I knew, someone was calling my name. "Betty! Betty!"

The voices seemed far away. There was a bright light. I realized it was the kitchen light.

"Are you okay, Betty? Are you okay?"

It was Bill. He was trying to get me to wake up. I finally sat up. I climbed up into a chair and sat while Bill finished drying the dishes for me. Both he and Ed were visibly frightened. Ed was lecturing us about "horsing around." I was a little dazed, but all right. However, this experience had a profound effect on me.

Our church was having special meetings: a revival. The guest evangelist was a fire and brimstone preacher who didn't mince words. I remember him saying, "You choose life or you choose death. God has laid before us life and death, but you must make the choice. Choose Jesus, or burn for eternity in the flames of hell."

The more he spoke, the more convicted I felt. It was as though I was the only one in church and he was speaking directly to me! Though I was only eight years old, the words seared deep into my soul. When he gave the altar call, I virtually ran down the aisle to the front of the church. That very night when I decided to choose Jesus, He touched my life mightily.

My family began to notice a difference in me. Like all children, I had fears. I was especially afraid of the dark. One day Mother had asked me to run down into the basement for something. As I started down those horrible, dark, dingy stairs, that same old fear attacked me. Suddenly, it seemed as if a shaft of light came down upon me, and a small voice within me said, "Fear not! I will never leave you or forsake you." At once the old fear was gone and was replaced with the assurance of His presence.

My mother even commented, "I can see our Lord Jesus has really changed your life." God is so good!

Several years later, many of the youth at our church had gone to a New Year's Eve prayer and praise service. After the service, my family invited the young people to our house to play games and have snacks together. There were about fifteen of us playing dominoes, monopoly, and doing puzzles. We served drinks and made popcorn. As the night wore on, one by one, everyone fell asleep, but Charles and I sat on the floor and talked. As dawn approached, I suggested we make breakfast for everyone. There were bacon and eggs in the refrigerator. I fried the bacon while Charles made the scrambled eggs and mixed the orange juice. It wasn't long until the smell of the bacon frying and the coffee perking roused everyone. After a hearty breakfast, the bleary-eyed crew went home.

Having had no sleep the night before, I fell into bed, falling asleep almost before my head hit the pillow, dreaming strange dreams.

In the dream, I stood in the back of our church wearing a wedding dress. Organ music played, and my friend fixed my dress. No one spoke. Suddenly it dawned on me that I didn't know who the groom was. I was anxious. As the door opened for me to walk down the aisle, I saw Charles waiting for me at the altar. My heart leapt. The joy in my heart was overwhelming. As I walked toward him, I awoke. It was mid-afternoon. I lay there peacefully asking myself, "What did I just dream? I felt so happy during the dream. What is happening to me? How could I dream this? We're just friends."

I made up my mind at that time that I would forget about this dream. I wanted nothing to jeopardize our friendship so I refused to dwell on it.

The following November, one of my favorite cousins, Jerry, got married. He had recently returned from a stint in the Marines where he had been stationed at Okinawa. His bride-to-be, Kathy, was planning the wedding and asked me to be a bridesmaid. She gave me a pearl earring and necklace set. We wore burgundy velvet gowns with a tight bodice and full-length skirt. We carried white rabbit-fur muffs. I was thrilled to be part of the wedding, and Jerry told me I looked all grown up.

In March of my junior year, my fingers literally bounced on the keys in my typing class. Totally into my work, I jumped when my teacher, Mrs. Collins, tapped me on the shoulder.

"Betty, there's a phone call for you in the office."

As I walked down the hall to the school office, I started to feel fear rising up from the pit of my stomach. Usually they don't allow students to have phone calls unless it is some kind of an emergency. I had never had a phone call at school.

When I arrived at the office, the secretary motioned me to a phone off the hook. I picked it up and said "Hello?" I was surprised to hear my mother's voice.

"Betty, I have some really bad news. Your cousin Jerry was in a bad car accident on his way to work this morning and he's in a coma right now."

She paused for a minute and added, "We really don't expect him to live."

I stood there with the phone in my hand saying nothing. I felt tears welling up inside of me.

"Honey, I've arranged for you kids to come home at lunch time and we'll all go to be with Aunt Vera and Mom."

"OK, Mom."

As I hung up the phone, I burst into tears and ran from the office. On my way back to class, I stopped in the washroom to compose myself. I quietly slipped back into the room, sat down at my typewriter, typed a few words and began to cry again.

Mrs. Collins came up to my desk and put her hand on my shoulder. "Betty why don't you just go home? I'll write you an excuse."

"Thank you, Mrs. Collins."

The wind stung my face as I walked home from school, yet I hardly noticed. A million thoughts raced through my mind. "He cannot die. He's been married only a few months."

I thought about Aunt Vera, one of my favorite people. We visited them every summer. Her two boys, Jerry and Peter came to our house for a couple of weeks and my brothers and I went to their house for a couple of weeks. We loved it. Being the only girl in our family, Aunt Vera spoiled me. She always sewed something for me and every year until I was in my teens, she would give me a magnificent doll. She worked at a doll factory. She taught me how to wear make up; she took me to movies; we laughed and played a lot together. During these times she had become my steadfast friend. We had developed a closeness that one seldom develops with an aunt. I knew that she would be torn apart over her son. I too, felt so sad.

We arrived in DeSoto to find Aunt Vera at the hospital. Her face was stained with tears. My mom embraced her and held her for a long time. We all prayed quietly as we kept our vigil. At about 11:00, our family left and went to Grandma's to sleep. We awoke the next morning to find that Jerry was gone. He never came out of the coma.

After the funeral, as we were ready to leave, Aunt Vera approached me. As she embraced me she whispered in my ear, "I hope we'll see a lot of you this summer, honey."

"I'll be here, Aunt Vera. I'll be here."

After we returned home, our lives slowly normalized as winter melted into spring and spring succumbed to summer. As soon as school was out, I packed my bags to go to Grandma's for the summer.

When I arrived in DeSoto, Aunt Vera was there waiting for me. We had a chance to walk and talk about Jerry. A mother's grief for a lost child will follow her to her own grave. Only time can dull the sharpness of loss. I was glad she still had Peter and Kathy.

During one of those summer evenings Aunt Vera asked, "Betty, how would you like to stay with us and finish your last year of school here? We would love to have you."

I actually thought it was a great idea. Aunt Vera told me that she and Mom had talked about it and they both thought it was a good idea. The gossip in Chester about Charles and I still ran rampant. Charles and I actually tried to avoid each other – even at youth events. It was very awkward. Mom and Dad thought my being away at this time might dampen the fiery tongues.

My family came for me that Friday. Before we got home, Mom reminded me about the church picnic that evening.

I had not forgotten. I thought to myself, "Charles will be there." I hadn't seen him for awhile. I really did miss him. I wondered what he would think about my being away for the whole school year.

That afternoon we packed a dinner and went to the church picnic. Although it was Friday the thirteenth, it was a perfect day for a picnic. It was hot, but not the excruciating heat that we often had this time of year.

We had to park a fair distance from the shelter house because so many people were there. As my mother began to unpack our picnic dinner with everyone else, she noticed that she had left the tablecloth in the car.

"Betty, would you mind running back to the car and getting the tablecloth?"

I quickly ran back to the car. Just as I was closing the car door, Charles arrived and parked nearby. He looked great. He wore khaki pants and a blue and turquoise-colored shirt with two buttons open at the collar.

I shouted to him, "Hi Charley! How are you?"

He smiled, "Hey, long time no see. Where've you been?" And he walked slowly toward me.

"At my grandma's. I'm just home for the weekend."

I stopped with him as he took a cooler box from his car. I didn't notice the sudden gathering of clouds right above us. Just when we both started toward the shelter, the clouds opened up with a quick downpour – big silent drops of rain. We bolted for the nearest tree – me with a tablecloth in my hand, and Charles carrying a cooler box. We both got pretty wet. We looked at each other and burst into laughter.

Suddenly he stopped laughing and looked deeply into my eyes. I wondered if something was wrong.

"Betty, I know that this is very serious, but I wonder, do you have any idea how much I love you?"

My heart raced. In an instant, my entire relationship with Charles transformed into what I had dreamed of. I looked directly at him and surprised myself by saying, "I hope it's as much as I love you."

He then put his hand under my chin, raised my face up towards his and kissed me very lightly on the lips. A surge of emotion rushed through my entire being. I knew right there in my heart that this was so right. There was no stopping it. We stood looking intently into each other's eyes. Time had no meaning.

The rain stopped. Just as suddenly, he broke the spell, "We'd better get back to the picnic. You go ahead."

Reluctantly, I left him standing there and ran to join the picnic. I can hardly remember the rest of the day. My mind kept replaying what we had just said to each other.

That evening, Charles stopped by to talk to my brother Ed about plans for the youth group on Sunday. I was on the front porch by myself when he left. My eyes met his.

He turned towards me after glancing around to make sure that we were alone. Then, he spoke. "Betty, I'm sorry. I was really out of line this afternoon. This will never work. No one will be able to accept our being together."

He must have read my face as my countenance dropped. "What was I thinking? You are so young, still in school. You must enjoy your school days. Go out and have fun. After you graduate, if we still feel the same about each other, we'll talk more then. You will be away in a new school with new challenges. Promise me that you will have a good year. Promise me that you will have fun, and date and enjoy your last year of school."

I stared at him in unbelief. Charles had just put the brakes on our relationship! But I knew, deep in my heart, that he was right. I reluctantly promised to do as he had asked, but I wondered if I could. I only promised to do it because I cared for him.

Living with my aunt was a good change for me. It helped take my mind off Charles and what he had said to me. Even though I was the new girl in school, I had made new friends already. I was settling in and enjoying school and my new surroundings.

Back in Chester, my parents said they missed me, but they were pleased that I was happy. However, other currents were sweeping through our home. I was not there to see that my father was becoming increasingly depressed.

On a Thursday morning during the third week in school in September, my dad left for work as usual. My mother kissed him good-bye and sent him on. About an hour after he arrived at work, he called my mother on the phone.

He came directly to the point as soon as Mom answered. "Kay, do you always try to do things for the good of other people?"

She was caught off guard by the question. "Well, I try to do that, honey."

"That's what I thought. Well, I have to go now. Remember, I love you."

"I love you too."

She shook her head as she hung up the phone wondering what that was all about.

After Dad hung up the phone, he reached into the drawer and took out a revolver. Perhaps he reflected for a few seconds, but then he placed the barrel to his right temple and pulled the trigger. Within a few minutes the local police responded to the noise and found his body. It was all over, just like that.

About fifteen minutes after that phone call to Mom, the door bell rang. When Mom opened the door and saw the police and our pastor, she knew what had happened. Her knees buckled and she fell into the arms of the pastor and began to sob softly.

At about 10:30 a.m. that same morning, my cousin Peter came to get me at school. I was in home economics class and was surprised when the teacher came and said, "Betty, you need to step into the hall for a moment."

I wondered...but I obeyed and walked out into the hall. I was shocked to see Peter standing there, his eyes big with fear. "Betty, you need to get back to your mom, right now." He took my arm and started walking.

"Hold on!" I said. "What's wrong? Tell me what's wrong!"

"Come, we'll talk on the way."

"No! What is it? You tell me what's going on!"

"It's your Dad. He..."

"What about my Dad?"

"He shot himself."

I was stunned. Suddenly I felt sick to my stomach. How could this be true? Why would he do this? I was numb!

When we got home Aunt Vera was there, home from work already, and I fell into her arms. We wept together for some time. She kept saying, "Betty, I'm so sorry, I'm so sorry!" We hardly spoke. Neither of us knew what to say

That week was one of the most difficult in my life. The death of a loved one is difficult enough to endure, but when a loved one commits suicide, questions, doubts and fears begin their torment of those left behind.

We all blamed ourselves. I thought that if I had just not gone to Aunt Vera's, it would have been different. Bill blamed himself for not being there for Dad, for not being closer to him. Ed wondered if he should not have taken more time to listen and talk to Dad when he would say something negative. Could we have gotten him to talk more about what he was thinking? What could we have done differently? Why didn't we see this coming?

From the time I was ten years old, Dad had often commented that we would be better off without him. I used to wonder what he meant. Mom would usually hug him and say, "You know I couldn't go on without you." I didn't know how to respond. It soon became apparent that Dad was down or moody a lot of the time. Mom wanted him to see a doctor, but when she spoke to him about it he became angry. She decided to spend more time praying about it. When he acted on his thoughts and actually took his own life, it was not a shock to her.

By the time the funeral was over, we were all mentally, physically, and emotionally spent. After everyone had left I spoke to my mother, "Mom, I need to stay here now. You're going to need me."

She took my hand, "No, honey, you really should go back and finish the school year there."

I pressed, "Mom, I need to be here with you! I really don't want to be away now."

She spoke softly but firmly, "Betty, I really want you to go back. I don't want you changing schools again in your senior year."

After I returned to De Soto, I sat down and wrote Charles a long letter questioning why my father had done this. His reply came in a few short days. Charles said that sometimes we cannot understand things that happen. We will not know until we cross over to the other side. Then he quoted a scripture, "My grace is sufficient for thee. For my strength is made perfect in weakness..."

As I lay in bed that night, I realized more than ever that I really was in love with him. I remembered that dream I had after the New Year's Eve party. But, just like Scarlet O'Hara, I decided, "I'm going to think about this tomorrow." I fell asleep.

One evening, Aunt Vera, too tired to cook, decided we would go out to eat. It was not often that she did this. Most restaurants were of the family type, serving regular home-style meat and potato meals. DeSoto had its own home cooking restaurant downtown. I don't even remember the name, but the food was pretty good.

After we had ordered and were waiting for the waitress to bring our meals, two men in navy uniforms walked in to be seated. One was white and the other was black. The manager of the restaurant came out and explained to them that they could serve the white sailor, but not the black one. It was just the "rule of the establishment."

About that time, our food was served. Aunt Vera stood up and said, "Kids, don't eat anything. We're leaving!"

As we headed for the door, Aunt Vera, hardly able to contain her composure, stopped and told the manager, "If this place isn't good enough to serve these men, it isn't good enough for me. We haven't eaten any of the food, and we're not paying for it either!"

With that she left the restaurant, never to return again. We went home that night to bologna sandwiches and cokes. The bologna tasted better than usual. I was so proud of my Aunt for the stand she had taken.

I finished the school year in DeSoto and graduated with honors. During this time I was active in school as I had never been in Chester. I was very popular and as a result I was chosen for different parts in two school plays. My aunt made my clothes and the costumes for the plays. I frequently went on dates with different boys, although I refused to get overly involved with just one guy. I went to the homecoming dance with a close friend and had a great time. At our graduation, I also went to our end of year dance with Richard, a close friend who respected my desire to be only friends. We went together with five other couples. One of my friends, Alison, asked my twin brother to go to the dance with her and after the dance we all went to her house and climbed up on the roof of their house and watched the sun come up. We had a lot of laughs.

After graduation, I returned to Chester. I was really looking forward to seeing Charles again.

Chapter 5

COMMITTED

When I returned to Chester that summer, my mother was busy with the settlement of my father's estate, preparing to move, and closing on another house in another town. Dad had left our family some money. Mom took what was there, sold our own home in Chester and was able to buy a large boarding house in Carbondale, a town about forty miles away. The house had about fifteen rooms that were suitable for renting. Each room was small, kind of like a dorm room with a single bed, a nightstand, and a desk. With a large university in town, we were pretty well guaranteed of tenants, at least during the school year. The rent that Mom collected on these rooms combined with my dad's Social Security provided enough income for us to get by.

Carbondale wasn't much larger than Chester, but the presence of the university there gave the town so much more of a cosmopolitan atmosphere that it may as well have been on a different planet from Chester. After we settled in I got a job at WINI Radio in Murphysboro as a secretary. Murphysboro was only about six miles from Carbondale so the commute was easy. I liked my job. There was lots of variety; I even got to record the weather at times. My brothers, Ed and Bill, were still living at home. Ed was in college, but Bill refused to go back to school, so he got a job at A & W Root Beer.

I missed Charles so very much. I had not seen him for some time. We had continually corresponded through the mail, but I really wanted to see him. Living in Carbondale, I never ran into him like I used to when in Chester. My thoughts turned to him continuously. With each letter he seemed to open his heart a little farther. I admired his depth of spirit and his devotion to our Lord. I found myself longing for his company. Life without him was empty, and seemed devoid of purpose.

During this time I lost my appetite. I was neither anorexic nor bulimic, but I never thought of food or eating. It just didn't appeal to me. I soon began to lose weight. As an adolescent I was always clear-skinned, without blemish. I now began to break out with acne. These changes did not escape my mother.

Finally she approached me, "Betty, I think maybe you should go see a doctor. I'm a little worried about you."

I shrugged my shoulders, "Ok, if you think it's best."

I was able to see a doctor the following week. After a few questions, the doctor asked me a very pointed question. "Are you having a relationship with a married man?"

Shocked, I shook my head emphatically. "No!"

"Well, it seems to me that something in your life has your emotions in an upheaval. Physically I can't find anything wrong with you. I think you need to figure out what is causing these emotional problems."

The doctor's advice caused me to step back and assess my feelings. It didn't take long to realize that the situation with Charles had to be resolved. I hadn't seen him in so long. Did he still care about me at all? Had he found someone else? How would I go about rebuilding, or finally severing this relationship?

Ed and Charles had become pretty good friends through their work together in the youth ministry. I'm sure that my mother put him up to it, but Ed invited Charles to visit one evening. Under that guise, Charles came to our house.

When he arrived, I again realized how much I had missed him. We found we had a lot to talk about. He was there for a few hours, but to me it seemed like just a few minutes. Then he was gone.

It was so good to see him, even though the time was short. He did say he would come again and I hung onto those words, eagerly anticipating his next visit.

He made several visits to our house that fall. The third time he came he began to boast, "I've been making quite a few pies lately at the club. I'll bet by now I can make one much better than you can."

Being the competitive person that I am, I could not let this challenge slip by. I retorted, "You're on! Let's start baking!"

"I don't know, Betty. My pies get rave reviews at the club."

"We'll see about that! Come on!"

He required no coaxing. He was ready for the challenge. My family thought this was great, because they would eat the pies and judge the contest.

Within minutes, the kitchen was full of flour and piecrust. We chatted endlessly about this and that, needling each other about how our crust was going to be better.

As we were rolling out our pie crust our hands inadvertently touched. I stopped rolling my dough. He was looking at me. I searched the softness of his eyes, looking for something. I saw a mixture of admiration and trepidation. Time stood still for that instant.

I couldn't contain my words. "Charles, we have to talk."

He turned away. "I know."

Suddenly the pie contest was forgotten.

I probed, "You remember when we were caught in the rain storm at the church picnic last year?"

"Every night and every day I remember it."

"Charles, my feelings haven't changed. I'm still in love with you."

He looked away for a moment, hesitated, and then answered, "I'm still very much in love with you. I...I just thought that you were young and impetuous at the time. I couldn't let myself believe it."

"Well, what are we going to do about it?"

Surprised by the directness of my question, he just looked at me speechless.

"Charles, I'm a wreck. I've been losing weight. Look at how my face is broken out! I really need you. I can't stand to pretend anymore!"

He stood there, looking stunned. He was shocked to find that I cared for him so much.

I continued, "If you really love me, don't you think we should get married?"

He didn't hesitate. "Betty, there's nothing I want more. But how could it work, here and now? I've always wanted the best for you. I've dreamed of getting married and providing a home for you. I cannot leave Chester now, and I'm not sure, right now, when I can leave."

"I don't think I can wait much longer, we have to do something."

"Yes, I know we do."

After a few moments of reflection he said, "You know, Betty, I've heard that in Canada they are much more tolerant of mixed marriages. I've heard that they are less prejudiced in general there."

"Really?" It was obvious that this wasn't the first time he had thought about this option.

"I don't know if it's true or not. I've just heard."

"But whether or not it's true, we need to do something now. I can't go on like this. It's beginning to affect my health."

"I've noticed that you've been losing weight. I've been concerned about you. Surely you know how much I love you, don't you?"

I nodded.

"We'll pray about this some more, and I want you to rest in God's love and please eat more food, just for me, okay?"

I smiled and he took me in his arms.

He kissed me lightly on the lips and left. He was so tender, so gentle, not at all aggressive—just loving. As he left I felt joy, peace, assurance, doubt, excitement, and relief all at the same time. I was swirling in emotions.

We were now engaged, verbally, that is. Now I looked forward to his visits with greater anticipation each time. No longer did Charles come under the guise of visiting Ed. He came to see me and my family knew it. Each time he came we planned a little more of our future. When the Christmas season arrived, he planned to spend some of his Christmas vacation with us. I bought him a sweater. It was tan, trimmed with leather piping and leather pockets. It also had leather on the elbows. It was beautiful. I felt so happy that I could get it for him.

When he arrived at Christmas, we opened gifts. When he opened his, he was overcome with emotion. He knew it was an expensive sweater. He knew that I had sacrificed to get it for him. He just didn't think that I cared that much for him. I was touched by his open emotion.

Now, standing here watching the television images of Lesotho, I realized I loved Charles even more passionately and tenderly than I ever had. I prayed, "Lord, you are my husband's strength and shield. In You, I can trust."

Chapter 6

MARRIED

S till on my knees, I looked up when the phone rang. The U.S. Embassy was calling. They were getting in touch with all the Americans that they knew were still in the country. Previously, some of the rebels had broken into the home of a Baptist missionary couple. The rebels tied them up and threw them in the trunk of their car. Then they drove the couple up into the mountains where they abandoned them. No place was safe.

The Embassy presented a plan of escape to me. They had hired some mercenaries to escort small groups to the border. The only catch was that I would have to get to the Embassy within the hour. Although only a few blocks away, getting there required crossing a major street where some of the heaviest concentration of fighting was going on. I told them that it just wouldn't work. They agreed to phone me later and emphasized I should stay low.

As I huddled on the floor, staying away from windows, I prayed and praised God and found my mind wondering to the time Betty and I began our plans to get married.

We prayed about it a lot and asked God to direct us. I wanted to be able to provide for my future wife and family. Currently, my mother and brothers and sisters depended on my income. If I married Betty, I was certain to lose my job. I just couldn't see a resolution–except maybe Canada.

All my life I had researched and read books about history and life in Canada. Perhaps, this was the answer. I decided to make an exploratory trip there and check it out myself. I shared my ideas with Betty. If my trip proved successful, she would meet me in Danville to get married. If not, well, we just didn't have a plan B.

We laid our plans before the Lord and agreed to meet in the square in Danville and then proceed to the church together. Betty called a Baptist minister there and explained to him why we needed someone from outside of our church to marry us. He said he would be happy to help us and glad to marry us.

I took a one-week vacation from work–something I had never done before. I drove through Detroit on my way and toured a Chevrolet plant. I was fascinated with the process of seeing a car made from beginning to end. Then I visited the proving ground. You couldn't go on the track, but you could view the cars being tested. They would come around the track and then disappear into nowhere.

After that I continued on to Windsor.

Windsor amazed me. I could stay wherever I wanted and eat wherever I wanted. I felt free to do as I pleased for the first time in my life. I knew then and there that Betty and I had a future together.

I called Betty. "Canada is everything I had hoped it would be! Lord willing, we'll meet in Danville."

Then I had a long drive, a good eight hours, to our designated meeting point at the courthouse in Danville, Illinois. The courthouse closed at 5 and I pulled into the parking lot at 4:45. Thank you Lord. Betty and her family met me there.

Inside the courthouse, racism confronted us once again. The clerk balked at giving us a license. He looke into the face of Betty's mother and said, "Woman, do you realize what you are doing here?" Betty's mother took charge, "Young man, you are paid to do your job. Not to give us your opinion. I suggest you do your job." The clerk shook his head, but he complied in the face of that determined woman.

From there we drove to the church together. Betty boldly rode in the car with me. When we arrived at the church, we were surprised when a black minister greeted us. He had lined up six of his deacons to witness the marriage. An organist played music softly in the background. The minister led us each to a room where we could dress. Betty wore a white silk dress and I wore my black suit. Betty's Mother and her brother Ed were our witnesses. Betty's twin brother took photos of the ceremony. We felt special and privileged to start out our married life in such an atmosphere. This experience provided us with a ray of hope and encouragement. When we stepped out of the church afterwards, a stunning rainbow greeted us. We stood there and held hands soaking it in and praising the Lord.

After our two-night honeymoon, I returned to Chester and Betty stayed in Carbondale. We told no one, including my family, about our marriage. I felt it was just too dangerous, especially for my younger brothers and sister. For the next year and a half, we met secretly once or twice a week. I couldn't always get away because of responsibilities to my family.

I asked Betty if she would like to come to Chester and meet me sometimes. She agreed, so we decided she could come to me after church on Wednesday nights. I asked her to pull into a car lot and drive all the way to the back and turn her lights off and wait for me there. I knew her church got out about 9pm and she would be here about 10pm. I saw her pull in. She was really glad to see me. We crept through the woods, crossed the road and went up through the brush on the other side and came out at my back yard. I lived alone in that old house. Usually there was little or no traffic to worry about there, however, there was one evening that a car came racing down the hill and we had to lay flat praying it would not see us. We repeated this procedure, going the other way when it was time for Betty to leave (just before sun up). Betty was really nervous about doing this and I was concerned about her driving home too. She related one incident of God's continual protection early one morning:

"I was driving home very slowly, crying out to God for answers. 'Why did we have to meet like this? Why could we not be just like any other couple in love? Why were people against us?' I was really getting into a good pity party. Then it came to me. God was richly blessing us. Charles and I had really gotten to know a lot about each other through our letters to each other. We were open and honest with each other. We shared our dreams, our deepest thoughts and so many other things. I was beginning to see clearly that we had to really be strong. We had to fight for our marriage and that made it much more special to us. We could not take each other for granted, because we had to fight for every moment to be together. Ours was not a relationship based on looks, or lust, but on friendship and now we were in love. Charles was my Spiritual leader and now he was my husband. I was beginning to realize that we were indeed richly blessed, very richly blessed. Many people do not have an opportunity to really get to know their partner until after they are married and then, too often, they don't like what they've got. I began to really praise God and I asked Him to forgive me for murmuring. I was almost home and looking in my rear view mirror, I noticed the same police car that I had seen over half an hour ago was still behind me. He never stopped me, he just stayed behind me. I guess he just wanted to make sure I got home okay. I started praising God for my escort home."

We knew we could not keep meeting like this so we planned that the following year, I would take my vacation with Betty to get a better look at Canada. Betty's mom also took a trip to Canada with Betty to make sure we wouldn't be living in a snow bank. We studied a map to determine where we might move. We didn't want to live more than eighteen to twenty hours away from Chester.

We wrote letters to many places in Canada. Only one place responded with more than tourist information. That place was Kitchener. The mayor himself responded.

Dear Mr. and Mrs. McGee:

Thank you so much for your interest in Kitchener. We are very proud of our community, for we feel that it has much to offer. I sympathize with your situation, and am sorry that you have encountered the difficulties that you have in your home country. I submit to you that you will not find the same attitudes in our community. You are more than welcome to settle here.

I have sent your job qualifications and addresses to a local employment agency. They should be in contact with you soon. I would encourage you to come and visit our community and see for yourselves what it is like. If and when you do come to visit, please stop by my office. I would look forward to making your acquaintance.

Sincerely:
Alfred R. Grimm, Mayor of Kitchener, Ontario

We decided right then and there it would be Kitchener. They made us feel welcome before we even arrived. And, that welcome continued through our entire time there.

True to the mayor's word, we received correspondence from the employment agency that our skills were greatly in demand in Kitchener.

At last, the time came for our vacation. Early one morning, I left home and headed north. Betty's family drove her about an hour north where we met and continued on to Canada together. After being married for fifteen months we finally had a real honeymoon.

It was wonderful to travel together, talking, laughing, and singing praises. We arrived in Kitchener late that night and found a hotel. We just checked into our room, as would any other married couple. No one told me that I couldn't stay because of my skin color.

In the excitement of the moment, we forgot to pay the manager. I went back and he said to me, "That's okay. I can tell newly-weds." This man was so warm and friendly towards us; he even recommended places to eat. He was Portuguese.

That week we had the time of our lives. We ate in restaurants together. We saw a movie together. We went bowling together. We walked through the park holding hands and no one seemed to notice that we were different! It was the exciting beginning of a new journey. When we went to church that Sunday we sat together as a married couple for the first time in our lives without being stared at. As we sang the first hymn, I looked over at Betty and saw tears of joy trickle down her cheeks. I had never experienced anything like this.

In between all of the fun we made time to meet with the man at the employment agency who had sent us the letter. He reminded us that we would need applications for immigration as well as medical exams and other forms. He recommended that we take care of those things while we were there. We thought that was a very good idea. There was much to do and many places to go. Usually processes such as this are a distasteful chore, but for us it was a chance to work together to build a dream. We thoroughly enjoyed every minute of it. We didn't mind the physical exams and the doctor we saw eventually became our family doctor. By the time we were ready to return to Illinois, all of our paperwork was completed and submitted. They told us it would take six to eight weeks to process the forms.

We returned to Illinois, each of us to our own homes. We never called each other directly for fear of the local operators listening in and spreading gossip. So, first thing Monday morning, Ed called and told me that Betty had received the immigration approval. We had three months to decide whether or not we were going to Canada. We decided to leave in two months. That would be enough time to get our affairs in order and to tie up any loose ends.

Chapter 7

CANADA

I knew that now was the time to tell my mother. I went to her house, just up the hill from my own. I usually went over there every day to help out, and to check up on things. I had been helping her financially for quite some time and provided guidance to the younger children as man of the house. I wanted to say goodbye properly and leave their affairs in good order.

I sat down with my mother. "Mom, you know how long I've talked about Canada. I was really impressed with the difference I experienced there. I've decided I want to move there."

Her face fell. "Do you really think that's a good idea? After all, you don't really know anybody up there, and you'll be all alone. And, what about us?"

"Jim is nearby. He'll step in. Another thing Mom; I've been married to Betty for over a year now."

She was speechless.

"Mom, I thought it was better for everyone that you and the rest of the family didn't know."

The hurt showed on her face, but she said nothing.

"I just wanted to protect you and the family. You know how it was when gossip was going around about us years ago, and how they wanted to take it out on all of us. I couldn't let that happen."

"I'm disappointed that you didn't tell me."

"I'm sorry, Mom. But, I still don't think it is safe. I don't want the younger kids to know. I don't want to put them in the position of defending me."

She understood, but I could see that it grieved her that she hadn't been told. "I'm happy you won't be alone. You know, we'll miss you."

I was blessed that for years afterwards we were able to continue to give her some financial support every month. In addition, shortly before we left, the IRS came after me because my tax claim for dependents for my brothers and sister wasn't documented properly. There was nothing to be done but pay the seven thousand dollars that the IRS demanded. I made arrangements to pay them off on a monthly basis.

On our moving day I rented the biggest U-Haul trailer I could find and left with what few belongings we had: an old upright piano, a sewing machine, a double bed, a card table with two folding chairs, and two wooden sitting chairs. We also had a few dishes, our clothing and some bed linens. What we had didn't even fill the trailer.

Then, I drove to Betty's house to get her and her things. Betty said a tearful goodbye to her mother and her brother. We got on the road at about midnight. For the first two hundred miles of our trip Betty wept. I began to have second thoughts about our decision: I had just left a good job; we were making a big move to a place we didn't know; would this be a round trip? I shook those thoughts out of my head and started talking to Betty about our future. Finally, my words got through to her and me. Gradually, she joined me in a discussion about our future together. Then we praised the Lord and sang songs. As the sun rose, so did our spirits, and so did our hope.

We arrived at my brother Don's house in Harvey, Illinois and slept most of the day. Don was the one person I had confided in about my love for Betty and I had said it only once. But, I hadn't told him we were married. However, when we arrived, they were not at all surprised and welcomed us with open arms.

We left Harvey in the wee hours of the morning and arrived in Kitchener that evening totally exhausted. We went straight to the hotel. The next morning, feeling more rested we started to look for a place to live. Among the ads was one for a lovely one-bedroom apartment in the upstairs of a home. We decided to look at it.

When we arrived at the home we met Mrs. Metcalf, the owner. She seemed polite enough. The apartment was perfect for us. It consisted of one bedroom, a sitting room, a kitchen and a bathroom. Outside the kitchen there was a lovely porch overlooking the neighborhood.

We paid the deposit and began to unpack. The next day I went out for job interviews while Betty stayed home to unpack.

I went on two interviews. The first job was for a straight night shift and they offered it to me. The second job was three weeks working days, then one week working nights–3 until midnight. They offered it to me, but I had to write an exam before being certified. Joyfully, I took it and called Betty.

"Betty?"

"Charles, where are you?"

"I got a job!"

"That's great! Where is it?"

"It's at the Ford dealer here in town. He took me on as a mechanic."

"When do you start?"

"About five minutes ago. I'll be home for supper, Okay?"

"I'll have something special for you."

"Great! Bye, I'll see you tonight."

"Bye, honey. I love you."

I decided to surprise Betty by coming home for lunch only to find her sitting on the top step, with our boxes not unpacked. Her tear-stained eyes looked up at me sadly. Obviously, something was very wrong.

"Betty?"

"Oh, Charles," she began to cry. "Charles, we can't stay here. Mrs. Metcalf came and gave our deposit back and said we couldn't stay. She even said that she didn't know if we were really married."

I knew we weren't moving. We had a contract. Mrs. Metcalfe was faced with change and I had to help her through it. Why, she didn't even know me yet! People can make a decision by sight, but that isn't good enough. You have to get to know people before you make a true decision. I had confidence that when she talked more with me, she would change her mind. I would go down and confront her. I told Betty, "Give me that deposit and hang up our marriage license!"

I knocked at her door. Mrs. Metcalfe answered but did not invite me in. With the deposit in hand I spoke to her at the door. "Mrs. Metcalf, my wife told me what you said today."

She stood silently, apprehensively.

"You were willing to rent the apartment to us yesterday, but you thought about my color and began to have second thoughts."

Still she stood and listened.

"Then, I'm sure, you began to worry about what neighbors would think, and nonsense like that."

Her face became more pensive. She back-pedaled. "Oh, I don't know what I was thinking."

I continued, "Well, I've paid you a deposit. I'm returning it to you because we are not moving. We've paid for a month and we will stay for a month. If you still have those fears after you've gotten to know me, we'll move, but not until you've seen the real me, and not just the color of my skin."

With that I placed the deposit in her hand.

"Oh, I had no right to do that," she said.

I turned to leave, but then stopped, "Why don't you come upstairs and join us for a cup of tea. Wouldn't that be a good start?"

She said, "Thank you. I'd love to."

I dashed back upstairs, "Honey, put on the tea pot. We're staying and Mrs. Metcalf is coming up to have tea with us."

In a few minutes she arrived. We laughed and talked together. When she left she was very much at ease and even invited us to her church that Sunday.

After that we became the best of friends. Mrs. Metcalfe would play piano and we would sing. She'd often come up for dinner. At that time, we had a pair of mynah bird salt and peppershakers. She saw them one day and laughed, "These look like me!" We nearly died laughing inside, because she was absolutely right. They did look like her! After that, I threw those shakers out.

Mrs. Metcalfe was getting up in years and found it difficult to back her car out of the garage without hitting the house or a tree. I've never seen anyone who could get their car sideways in such a narrow driveway, but somehow Mrs. Metcalfe did. I developed the habit of backing her car out for her every day that she needed it. And, we stayed in that apartment with her until we built our first home two years later.

Now, sitting here in a war zone, I thought about how God had brought us through all those human land mines. I was sure that God could handle a few mortar shells and automatic weapon fire. The phone rang, and I reached for it. Maybe it was the Embassy with a new plan. I heard Betty's voice.

Chapter 8

BLESSINGS

"Hello?" I was stunned to hear Charles' voice. I was also thankful that the phones were still working. That's usually one of the first things to go out at any sign of trouble.

"Charles, what are you still doing there? It's all over the news, the trouble in Maseru!"

"It started early this morning," he replied, "and I have not been able to find a way out yet. But, the American Embassy is trying to get me out. Everything here is burning. The sky is thick with black smoke and everything smells of it. It's like night time already."

We prayed together over the phone, thanking God for His protection and His divine wisdom. After we hung up, Barry, Tina, little Sharon and I began to pray and intercede. Thank God, I had my faith and my children. I wasn't alone. God had provided every step of the way–even for our first church home in Canada.

After years of a secret courtship, a secret marriage, and everything hidden, we were finally able to come out into the open and become a normal couple. We didn't have to sneak around to be together. We lived together—openly. Shortly after Charles secured his employment, I found a job. To many people this would sound like a boring life. To me, it was heaven.

Now that we were settled into our apartment and our jobs, we started to look for a church. We asked God to direct us to the right church. The following Thursday evening after work, we drove around town looking and discovered Glen Acres Baptist Church. We also noticed that the name of the pastor was the same name as our pastor at home.

Charles and I just looked at each other. We decided to go to the pastor's home and see if we could meet him.

We knocked at his door, and Charles said, "Hi, I'm Charles McGee and this is my wife, Betty. We're new to Kitchener and we were looking for a church."

It was still a little difficult for us to introduce ourselves as husband and wife considering our past experience in the U.S. We always expected disapproving looks from people. However, this man smiled, extended his hand to shake our hands and warmly invited us in.

He showed us to the living room. It was a small room but quite cozy.

"Please, sit down."

He left the room for a few minutes and returned with a lovely, dark-haired woman.

After introductions all around his wife went out to make tea. We sat with the pastor.

He started, "So tell me something about yourselves. Where are you from and why did you choose Glen Acres?"

We took turns in telling him of our backgrounds in Southern Illinois and as we finished, Charles said, "I don't know why we chose this church. We prayed about it and I think that this is where God is leading us."

"Wow, that's quite a story. I feel really blessed that God sent you to us."

Just then, his wife came back into the room with a steaming pot of tea and some cookies.

After tea, we prayed together and prepared to leave.

Just as we were about to leave, the Pastor stopped and asked, "Do you have a little more time this evening?"

Charles answered, "Sure, what do you have in mind?"

"Well, the choir is practicing tonight. Maybe I could introduce you to some of our people before Sunday."

"That would be great!" I answered.

We proceeded to the church where the choir was rehearsing the Hallelujah Chorus. When they paused, the pastor introduced us. The director was a skinny little lady. She didn't weigh 90 pounds and talked 90 miles a minute–non-stop.

The director said, "Betty, are you soprano or alto, and Charles, tenor or bass?"

I answered, "Both."

Charles said, "Bass"

"Good, we need a bass and a soprano!"

She handed us sheet music, which we had never used before–only hymnbooks. Surprised, we took our places. The music began and we were immersed!

After the rehearsal, we all had coffee. Everyone was warm and friendly. After we got home that night, one of the couples from the choir, John and Ann, showed up at our door.

John said, "We'd like to take you out for coffee."

We agreed. (We drank a lot of coffee that day.)

While we were eating together they asked us if we would be in Canada for Christmas, which was less than five weeks away. We said yes. We were so surprised when they asked us to have Christmas with them. John had a pharmacy company with three stores that did very well. They lived in a really nice area of Kitchener and had no children. John and Ann were so down to earth and so loving. They opened a lot of doors for us and we formed a friendship that night that has lasted to this day. They even came to visit us in Africa–a wonderful adventure where we camped along the Zambezi River in Botswana. We had Christmas together with them and their family every year thereafter for thirteen years, when our children came along.

I was so grateful. When we left Illinois, I had never felt so alone. I left a busy life filled with church activities and friends. In Canada, we knew no one. Now, after such a short time, we had a whole new life filled with church, work and new friends. God had filled every void and then some.

Both of us became very involved in serving in church. We both taught Sunday school for years. We both sang in the choir. We were both youth leaders. The pastor and board asked Charles to serve as a deacon, so he did that as well. We worked hard but we worked together.

One year, Charles taught Sunday school to a new class of six-year-old boys. He was fond of the children and the class was a joy to teach. The boys were eager to learn, always asking questions. Their innocence and inquisitiveness provided lots of good fun.

Several months after Charles began to teach the class, we received an invitation to lunch from Ricky's parents. We enjoyed the food and the fellowship very much. They were a delightful family.

After dinner, we retired to the living room for tea and more time to chat. It was then that Ricky's father told us how they had tried to prepare their son that a person of a different type would be teaching this class. They knew that Ricky was very inquisitive, and they didn't want him to embarrass them or Charles. They instructed Ricky that if he saw something different about the teacher (because Charles was black), he must just come home and talk to his parents about it.

The first Sunday came and the boy said nothing to his parents. The second Sunday came and still the boy said nothing about his teacher. The third Sunday went by without any comment from Ricky. Finally, his father spoke to him, "Son, did you enjoy Sunday school?"

Ricky replied, "Yes, Daddy."

Then his father pressed, "Do you have a new teacher?"

Ricky nodded.

Finally his father said, "Did you notice anything different about your teacher?"

Ricky shrugged, "No."

His father continued, "Really, nothing?"

Ricky became adamant. "No, Dad!"

His parents assumed that Ricky wasn't in Charles' class until they actually asked him his teacher's name.

"Mr. McGee."

We all laughed uproariously together. It's true that whoever does not receive the kingdom of God as a little child will by no means enter it. And, Ricky was our proof.

Because of the complexities of our life, Charles and I didn't have children for our first ten years together. We just didn't consider it. However, much of our ministry was with children. They were so open, so eager to learn, so eager to live life to the fullest and were always a source of joy to us.

After praying for some time about it, we felt God leading us to keep foster children. To begin with, we were assigned children between the ages of five and sixteen. Although fostering was a very rewarding experience, giving them back to their parents became very difficult.

Eventually, when a social worker came to collect one of the children to return to their home, she said to us, "The two of you are so good with children, why don't you adopt a baby of your own?"

We had thought that because of our status as a mixed race couple, we wouldn't be eligible to adopt. But she said, "No. Go ahead and fill out the paper work."

When we went to the adoption agency, our caseworker told us that it would take at least a year–maybe two or three.

Since we had been married for over ten years, she also recommended that we take a five to six year old child.

We didn't disagree with anything that she said. So we didn't specify anything, but we knew in our hearts that God had a baby for us.

We shared our plans with some of our Christian friends. They became prayer partners with us as we continued to seek God in bringing the right child to us in His perfect timing. We knew that God was in complete control.

Nine months passed. Then, a different social worker came as a customer to the garage. She spoke to Charles about her car and then shared an amazing thing. She said their agency had this darling little mixed race baby boy. She wondered if we knew of anyone who might have a good home for him because he was hard to place. Whites didn't want him because he wasn't white. Blacks didn't want him because he wasn't black. Charles was amazed that she did not know we had applied to adopt a child. He shared this information with her. She became very excited and told Charles to go home and prepare for the baby boy who would be with us soon.

We transformed our guest bedroom into a nursery that very weekend. We bought furniture, put up a mobile, purchased baby clothes and so on. We wallpapered and laid carpet. We were so exhilarated that our energy never stopped. The agency came and inspected the room on Monday. Afterwards, our caseworker said we could come and get our son that Friday.

I was bubbling over with excitement. I had already arranged to take a six-month leave of absence from work. On Monday, the last day before my leave I said my good-byes and started to head out the door to my car. Just before I came to the back door, someone grabbed me and pulled me into a conference room where all of my fellow employees were gathered. "SURPRISE!" they all chorused. I was shocked! It was a baby shower! Everyone had gotten together to plan it.

Such a blessing! There were diapers, baby clothes…everything we needed, including a beautiful high chair. I walked out of work that night feeling completely overwhelmed and blessed.

The next day we went to the adoption agency where we waited fifteen minutes; the longest of my life. We said very little to each other during those few minutes. Finally, we saw a lady come through the door carrying a little baby in a little white hood and we saw his big dark eyes, wide open and looking at us. Sure enough, right after that, our caseworker came in holding our son. My eyes filled with tears as I looked into his little face. This was our son, Charles Barry. He had straight black hair and big, beautiful brown eyes. There were five fingers on each little hand at the end of arms that seemed to be reaching out to us. I know he was smiling at us. I took him in my arms and held him close. As I held him for the very first time, it was as if I had given birth to him myself.

I whispered softly into his ear, "Barry, I'm your mommy and this is your daddy. We've waited for you for so long. The first thing I want you to know is that Jesus loves you and is blessing you. And I will love you forever." Charles took him from me to keep my tears from getting him wet. Barry's little hand reached up and touched Charles' cheek.

God is so wonderful to us. We praised Him and thanked Him for this perfect little boy, our son.

We kept him to ourselves for a few weeks and he adjusted well. The first night or two, he whimpered a couple of times and, of course, we sprinted out of bed to attend to him. Our son brought us more joy every day. He was always so happy. He greeted us every day with a big smile. He took pleasure in just about everything: eating, sleeping, his bath time, and our walks in the park. It was such a blessing to watch him grow every day and experience new things. One of his favorite things was to cuddle up on our laps while we read to him. One day as I was holding him, I had a vision of him as an evangelist–just like John the Baptist. Later on in Africa, another pastor spoke the same prophecy over him.

From time to time our caseworker would stop by, as was required by our adoption agreement. One day she informed us, "We're looking for a second child for you. Would you like another boy, or is your heart set on a girl?"

I was shocked because we were quite content. We had really not expected, or even hoped for another child. Barry had brought us all the happiness we had ever dreamed of.

I replied, "Well, we really hadn't thought about it. Can we get back to you?"

"Of course! Think about it, and let me know soon. Okay?"

"Okay, we will." I replied.

Charles and I looked at each other. We decided we would pray about it.

We wondered; could we handle another child? Would there be enough love to go around? Only God knew those answers. After much prayer, we felt led to ask for a girl. We knew that God would have the perfect child in His perfect timing. And if there was not to be another child for us, we could accept that, too.

We didn't ask for, but looked for signs from God. And, He gave us one.

The phone call came. We had a girl. What amazed us was that her birthday was one year and one day after Barry's. We knew that God was speaking to us. She had been born prematurely and we had to wait until she was six months old before we could bring her home. They wanted to check her very closely for any possible problems before they placed her. We decided to call her Christina Marie; Tina for short.

The time came. Taking our son with us, we went to collect our daughter. He was so excited about being along that it was all he could talk about: his baby sister.

We had to drive to Toronto to get her. It was January 31, the day after Charles' birthday. There was black ice on the road and accidents littered the way. It was frightening, but that day, nothing could stop us, even though we had to drive 35 miles per hour the entire way.

When we arrived, Tina was wearing a beautiful red dress with lace around the edges. She was fine-boned, small and almost frail. She looked at us with her huge brown eyes fringed with long, dark eyelashes that looked like spider legs down her cheeks. Little dark ringlets of curls covered her head. We took turns holding her and talking to her. Barry wanted to kiss her all the time. But she just looked at us, and kept looking at us, as if she were uncertain, maybe even a little frightened. But she never cried. We signed all the paper work and headed home with our new baby.

Barry fell asleep. I was holding Tina and talking to her. I told her how very special she was and how happy we were that God brought her to us. I also told her that we would love her forever. As we neared home, I was fluffing her clothes up when I was shocked to see a huge umbilical hernia sticking up and out, looking really awful. Charles and I decided to stop at our doctor's office on the way home.

The doctor said that Tina's condition was dangerous and she needed surgery as soon as possible. He explained that part of the intestines was in the hernia and this was causing her pain. We could see as he examined her, she cried when he moved the hernia. It was a Friday afternoon, so he scheduled it for the following Monday morning.

When we arrived home, our neighbors and friends came over to see this new blessing that was now a part of our family. They lovingly brought food and gifts for our new daughter.

The following Monday, it was time to go to the hospital for the hernia operation. Charles agreed to take care of Barry while I went to be with Tina at the hospital. For two days and three nights I stayed at the hospital, praying over her, singing to her, and rocking her. During that time, Tina began trusting me.

After a few days' recovery, Tina was doing so well, we took her home. Barry, who was happy to see her, kept bringing her his toys. Tina was a good baby and easy to care for. She didn't eat as eagerly as Barry, but she loved being held. When I would put her in her bed, she played with her feet until she fell asleep.

When Charles arrived home from work that evening he immediately went to see Tina. However, she was frightened of him and cried when he came near. I was very concerned about this, but Charles assured me that it was a temporary thing. Sure enough, after about a week she began trusting him, too. She loved to have Daddy hold her and tuck her into bed. Until she was five or six years old, she wouldn't let Charles or me out of her sight. If anybody else tried to pick her up, she would have none of it.

Charles always woke early to pray and seek the Lord's direction for the day. The first thing he did was to check on the kids in their rooms. When he went to check on Barry one particular morning, he found an empty crib. Concerned, but not yet panicked, he began to check throughout the house. First he went to the family room to see if Barry was watching television. Then he checked the front door and the back door to ensure that they were still locked. They were. He then methodically checked every room in the house, including the closets, all to no avail.

Finally he came to me at the side of the bed and gently woke me. "Honey, I don't want to scare you, but I can't find Barry anywhere. He's not in his crib."

I leapt out of bed and checked his room. Sure enough, he was not there. I ran to the doors to check the locks. They were still secure.

Charles said, "You're doing everything I've already done. I don't know where he could be."

Now, both concerned and not sure what to do next, we returned to our room to pray and ask God for guidance and wisdom. Horrible thoughts were trying to attack my mind.

As we were praying, Charles vaguely remembered that he had heard a bump during the night. Immediately we both looked under the bed to see Barry lying on his back, fast asleep.

One morning I left them in their rooms to get dressed. Barry was about three years old and Tina was two. I went to the kitchen to prepare breakfast. When they didn't come for breakfast after a reasonable time, I went back to check on them. As I walked back to their bedrooms I heard delirious laughter coming from our room. "Uh-oh," I said to myself, "What are they up to now?"

When I entered the room I saw the two of them jumping on the bed with my striped knee-high stockings and only their underwear. My stockings completely covered their little legs. They didn't even notice when I came in. Such a sight! I was laughing so hard I could hardly hold the camera to get the snapshot for their picture album.

When Tina was about two, she began to develop a strange illness. She would be fine during the day, but at night she would grow ill, often sick to her stomach and would go into labored breathing. As the condition persisted, we took her to our family doctor. He decided to give her some tests, which would require hospitalization. So there were several stays in the hospital.

Once when we came to visit her in the hospital, we saw her through the nursery window taking a bath. She was sitting in a little pink bathtub washing herself and singing, "Jesus Loves Me." We tapped on the window and waved at her.

She looked up startled. Then she looked upset. She said, "Don't look at me! I'm bathing!"

Of course we respected her wishes. Stepping away from the window, we waited outside the door. Within minutes she burst out of the door, completely naked, and jumped into her father's arms. We couldn't contain our laughter. She just looked at us and laughed along with us.

Chapter 9

ANGELS GUARDING

The doctors informed us that she had severe allergies to trees, grass, and animals. These allergies were causing severe mucous asthma. As part of her therapy, the doctors prescribed a regimen of breathing exercises, which she faithfully performed on a daily basis. She would lie on her back with knees bent, take very deep breaths, hold them in and exhale slowly. These exercises helped to develop her lung capacity and therefore somewhat alleviated the symptoms of her asthma.

We also found that swimming helped her a lot. I remember when we went to the YMCA for her first swimming lesson. At her age, I was required to go into the water with her. We were just walking into the swimming area and Tina let go of my hand and ran to the pool. She leapt into the water in the deep end where she immediately went under. I immediately jumped in after her. When we both came out of the water she sputtered, "Mommy! That was fun! Can we do it again?"

Being so fearless, she learned to swim very quickly.

A few months later, our family was having lunch together in the kitchen. Charles was getting ready to take Barry to nursery school, while I was planning to stay with Tina.

I asked her to stay inside while I went outside with Barry and Daddy to say good-bye. I suggested she start doing her breathing exercise while I was outside.

It seemed that I had just left the house when I felt a little hand on the back of my leg. When I turned, Tina was standing there.

I was slightly perturbed and very curious as I said to her, "Honey, what are you doing out here?

She replied, "Mommy, there's a lady in the living woom."

After a quick good-bye to Charles and Barry, I took Tina's hand to help her back into the house. My mind was racing! A lady in the living room? How is this possible? How did Tina ever get outside by herself? She had never been able to handle this door alone. What had she been up to?

We walked up the stairs to the door. When I opened the door, I saw all these sparkly things on the carpet. What was this? I carefully picked up a piece to have a good look at it.

Tina persisted, "Mommy, Mommy! See the pretty lady?"

I half ignored her as I puzzled over the pieces of broken glass in my hand. Where could it have come from? I picked Tina up in my arms. She was smiling and looking away from me. I began to walk carefully into the house, toward the kitchen. As I went, there was more broken glass all around me. But where did it come from? I looked at the ceiling and found my answer.

The kitchen light globe, a huge round ball of glass, had fallen, hitting the table on the way down and breaking into thousands of pieces of glass. As I surveyed the floor, I looked at where Tina had been lying, doing her exercises. My heart skipped a beat as I beheld a large, dagger-shaped sliver of glass, stuck in the floor. I could hardly believe my eyes.

Still concerned about a stranger being in my house, with Tina in my arms, I cautiously moved to the living room calling as I went, "Hello, is anyone there? Hello?"

I looked at Tina, "There's no one here, Honey. I don't see anyone."

"Where did she go, Mommy?"

I wasn't sure how to answer her. I sat down on the sofa with her on my lap and asked her to tell me all about it.

She replied, "the pretty lady came and took me outside."

I held her close to me and prayed with her. I recalled the Psalm, "No evil shall befall you, nor shall any plague come near your dwelling. For He shall give His angels charge over you, to keep you in all your ways."

I explained to her that each one of us have angels that look after us and take care of us. I told her that she was a very special little girl, because she had gotten to see her angel. Charles and I still praise God for His goodness. We are grateful to God that Tina was not hurt.

Our son, Barry was always curious and eager to learn. Sesame Street on television was always one of his favorites. When we enrolled him in nursery school at age three he flourished, enjoying it more each passing day. He was constantly full of questions. Charles could do no work around the house without Barry right beside him, helping and asking questions. He frequently tried to see how things worked by taking them apart. And when it came to LEGOs, he was the master.

One evening after a particularly busy day, we put the children to bed early hoping to have some quiet time of prayer and some time to ourselves. Suddenly the lights went out. There was an odd crackling sound and a bluish light coming from the hall. Just as suddenly, the lights came back on. I could not imagine! What on earth could it be? I detected a strange pungent smell. Charles ran down the hall, straight to Barry's room with me right at his heels.

I will never forget what we saw as we entered the room. There was Barry, sitting up in bed with his scissors in his little hands. His hands and pajamas were black. His eyes were as big as saucers. I ran to him.

Charles stopped me and yelled, "Don't touch him!" Then he turned to Barry and said, "Barry, honey, don't move! Don't move a muscle. I'm going to unplug the lamp."

The minute that Charles unplugged the lamp I ran to Barry and took him in my arms. The scissors were still in his hands. They were special children's scissors with rubber handles. In the scissors I saw the neatest little hole where he had cut the wire. He did not even get shocked. He told us of a big blue flash, and then smoke–a lot of smoke.

The cause of the accident was a big happy face lamp right next to his bed. He was curious about the plug in the socket and the wire leading to the light and what would happen if the wire were separated from the light. So he decided to cut it. Amazingly he was not hurt at all, just scared.

We had a bit of a mess from the smoke, but we were grateful to God that he was not hurt. Barry, on the other hand, learned to ask more questions before experimenting.

Tina at about three years of age was a very happy, but determined child. When she saw something she wanted, she went after it, without thought of the consequences. She was also a little bit possessive and very protective of her older brother.

On a sunny summer day, the children and I were at the park. They were playing at the playground, going down the big slide. Tina went first, followed pretty closely by Barry. After Tina reached the bottom she waited for Barry. In an instant, he came flying down the slide and slowed at the bottom where the slope flattened out. Before he could get off, another little boy flew into him, hitting Barry in the back with the flat of his shoes. As quick as a flash, Tina jumped onto the slide ready to hit the boy to protect her brother. Fortunately, we were quicker than she was. I restrained her and convinced her that it was just an accident, and she should never hit. But she felt completely justified in attacking the little boy who ran into her brother. Tina has been protective of our family to this day.

After Tina's bath one evening, while she was getting ready for bed, Charles arrived home from work. We were still upstairs. Charles came to the bottom of the stairs and shouted, "Hello?"

I shouted back, "We're up here, honey!"

Tina ran to the top of the stairs to see her daddy. She started slowly walking down the stairs. Having taken a few steps up to meet her, Charles said to her, "Come, Honey!"

He was holding his hands out to her. He had expected her to come on down the stairs. He was most surprised when she took a big jump and leapt into his arms, knocking him back against the front door. It was only the door that kept them both from falling.

I was struck by her faith. With one word, she leapt into her father's arms. She knew that he would catch her. She knew that she was safe. She knew full well that her daddy loved her and would always take care of her.

I pondered on how much more our Heavenly Father loves and cares for us. I recalled how Peter left the boat during a violent storm and walked on water when Jesus said, "Come!" He only required one word from his Master to step out of the boat.

I pray that we as God's children will take that leap of faith and know that God is always more than enough in every situation.

Occasionally, I worked on Saturdays in a small town about twenty minutes from home. On one such morning, Charles took the children and drove me to work. After leaving me at work they headed for home. Just as they turned onto the street where we live, a wasp flew into the window and hit Charles in the throat. Then, it fell down into his shirt and began stinging him. Charles stayed calm while driving, all the time trying to pull the wasp out of his shirt to kill it. Finally, he succeeded and laid it on the dash of the car as he pulled into our driveway. Strangely, he noticed that there were huge colored balls bouncing in the light of the windscreen before his eyes. At the time he thought it was a funny reflection of the sun on the windscreen.

As Charles climbed out of the car he also noticed that his body seemed to be getting very heavy and it was becoming more difficult to move his legs. After taking the children out of their car seats he took them into the house. Suddenly he felt sick to his stomach. He went downstairs to the bathroom where he collapsed, hitting his head on the wall. The next thing he saw was Barry and Tina looking down at him. He thought, "Why are they upside down?" (He did not realize he had fallen.) "Where am I? What's happening?"

Tina was crying and screaming. "Daddy, Daddy, Daddy! Get up Daddy!"

Barry leaned down, right in Charles' face and said, "Daddy, are you okay?"

Finding it very difficult to speak, Charles finally gasped, "Barry, go next door and get help!"

Within minutes an ambulance with paramedics arrived. They loaded Charles onto a stretcher and struggled upstairs with him, out to the ambulance. One of the paramedics teased him, "The next time you're not feeling well and go to the bathroom, please go to the one upstairs!"

As the ambulance sped to the hospital, the paramedics continued to work on him. They kept questioning him, "What happened to you, sir? Do you remember anything?"

Charles finally gained enough strength to say, "A bee stung me"

Our neighbors called me at work and told me that Charles had been stung and had collapsed at home. They told me to leave work and meet him at the hospital. They assured me that they were watching Tina and Barry, and would continue to do so until I returned home. I was stunned.

I had no idea how I would get home. Before I had time to think, some of my co-workers arranged my transportation to the hospital. The ride seemed to be taking forever. I began to wonder if we would ever get there. All the time I was praying and clinging to the word of God. I had to keep my eyes on the Lord, knowing that He was my strength.

When we arrived at the hospital emergency room, the doctor walked straight up to me. He said, "It was touch and go, but your husband is just fine now. I want to keep him over night and observe him. He's been through a lot. If all is well when I see him tomorrow, then you can take him home."

I mumbled, "Thank you, Doctor. May I see him now?"

"Certainly," he replied, and took me to Charles.

I was taken aback when I saw Charles with all of those tubes hooked to him. He looked so tired. As I took his hand I asked, "How are you, honey?"

He began to relate his experience to me. He said that as he arrived at the emergency room they kept shouting at him, "Breathe, sir, you've got to breathe! Come on now, breathe!"

He said it seemed as if he was watching them work on his body. They were all talking at once and seemed to be so busy. They gave him some kind of injection while continually telling him to breathe. They kept speaking to him. They gave him another injection. Charles found himself wondering, "What are they so upset about?"

He felt so at peace, but they continued to work on him frantically. When he finally opened his eyes, the doctor said, "Well, sir, it's good to have you back. You seem to be breathing nicely now."

Having made sure that Charles was all right, I returned home to find two very excited children.

Barry was bubbling over. "Mommy, Mommy, Daddy went to the bathroom and we heard a big boom." (They had heard him hitting his head against the wall.)

I held them close and reassured them that Daddy was fine. We prayed together, and then told them that we could bring Daddy home tomorrow.

The following day was Sunday. After church we all went to the hospital to find Charles sitting up in bed waiting for us to come and take him home. Barry and Tina were excited to see Daddy again, doing so well. We rejoiced in the Lord's mercy. God had been so faithful to us. He knew the desires of our hearts before we even asked.

And now, all these years later, Barry and Tina continue to bring us joy, even in dark hours like these.

Chapter 10

THE CALL

As the fighting showed no sign of letting up, I read Psalm 46:1, 'God is my refuge and strength, a very present help in trouble.' And then verse 10: 'Be still and know that I am God.' These words brought me comfort.

I continued to praise God. I knew that He was the only one who could help me now. A high wooden fence surrounded our property, and a locked privacy gate controlled access to the driveway. Around mid afternoon a Land Rover came up to our gate and honked loudly. I saw it and wondered if it held rebels who would barge right through my gate and come in. Within minutes a man climbed on top of the vehicle and yelled, "Moruti Charles!" (Moruti means pastor.)

I looked more closely and saw that it was my friend Pastor Dickson from Zoë Bible Church, whom we'd worked with for so many years. I cautiously slipped out to the gate.

"Pastor Dickson," I said. "It's good to see you."

"Moruti Charles, I just wanted to see if you were okay or if you needed help."

"Well, I am fine so far."

"What about Me' Betty?"

"She and Tina are back in America."

"Good! It's really very, very bad!" He continued, "Moruti Charles, I want to try to get you out of Lesotho, but I'm not sure how."

"Well, at the embassy they told me to stay put. They are trying to get me out. I don't want to get killed trying to escape."

He put his hand through the fence and I clasped it looking at him. There was no fear in his eyes. He trusted God.

"I'll pray for you," he said.

"And I'll pray for you."

With that I went back into the house. God had called us here, and wouldn't abandon us. I reflected back on how we ended up in southern Africa.

We had been serving God faithfully in our Kitchener church and I was often asked to preach, but we hungered for more. We were not sure what was lacking. I had a good job. We had two beautiful babies. We had two cars. We owned our lovely three-bedroom home. We had so much to praise God for, but something was missing.

We had moved from Glen Acres Baptist Church to Evangel Missionary Church a few years earlier. One Sunday as we were listening to the sermon, we noticed something different. The pastor spoke with more power, a greater anointing, and more passion. After the morning service, we spoke to the pastor and invited him and his wife to our home after the Sunday evening service.

That evening after tea and a light snack we began to talk. They cautiously taught us about the baptism of the Holy Spirit. This was all new to us. We had heard little of the baptism of the Holy Spirit, although there is much written about it in the books of Acts and Ephesians. After the pastor and his wife received the baptism of the Holy Spirit, they explained how they began to pray in tongues and to praise God continually. It was as if they had fallen in love with the Lord all over again. We clearly saw the change. It was so good to be with them and see the love of God and the joy of the Lord that was now so evident in their lives. It was certainly evident in his preaching too. Before they left, we prayed and praised God together for His many gifts to us.

In the ensuing weeks, we spoke often about the pastor and his wife and the dynamic change we saw in them. We began to feel that we should rededicate our lives to the Lord. We wanted God to be the Lord of our lives in every area. We prayed together and told God that we were willing to do whatever He wanted us to do and go wherever He wanted us to go.

A few months later, we received a letter from the Mennonite Central Committee (M.C.C.) asking us if we would consider serving with them on the mission field. This letter came as a complete surprise to us. Then we remembered what we had prayed. We were willing to do and to go wherever He wanted. We decided to respond.

However, as Betty and I talked further, we felt that we were right where we were supposed to be. I had started a new job driving a truck and making very good money only three months prior to this. I had wanted to drive a truck like this for quite some time, so we felt the job had been an answer to prayer. However, because of the commitment we had made to God we agreed to an interview with M.C.C.

At our interview, the first thing that I asked was how they came to write us about serving with them. The interviewer, Mr. Scott, told us that one of the youth we had worked with years ago went as a volunteer with M.C.C. When asked if they knew of any people who would be willing to serve, this young man's wife recommended us. The folks at M.C.C. also mentioned that this couple had spoken very highly of us.

As we talked further, Mr. Scott told us about the need to train tractor mechanics for the government in Lesotho. He ended our interview by asking us to pray about it and to come back and see them next week. I thought, "This couldn't be God. He is not the author of confusion." And yet, Betty and I both felt our spirit leap when we heard the name Lesotho.

I had finally gotten the job I had been praying for all of my life. It paid very well, and I was driving trucks locally. That meant I could be home at night and on the weekends. But, I continued to pray. I told God, "You will have to let me know, specifically, if you want me to do this."

On our way out the door, Betty reminded me that God had spoken to her at the age of fifteen that she and her husband would serve as missionaries in Africa. I knew that but had forgotten it and I'm sure that's why our spirit within us leapt when they spoke of Lesotho.

I suggested that we go to the library and see what we could find out about Lesotho. We found that Lesotho, formerly Basutoland, was a small nation completely surrounded by the nation of South Africa. Books referred to it as the "Kingdom in the Sky" because of its high elevation and mountainous terrain. The lowest point in the country was 1,400 meters above sea level, nearly a mile high! The land area of the entire nation was about the same as that of Maryland. Although it was in Africa, it wasn't in the tropics. The summers could be hot, but the winters could also be cold. The capital city was Maseru, situated on its northwest border with South Africa. The vast majority of people there spoke a language called Sesotho, but English was the second language. The more we read, the more we became convinced that this calling could be of God.

When we returned again to meet with the mission they told us that the Lesotho opening was closed. Instead, they asked us about pasturing a church in Montreal. Again, we agreed to pray about it.

I wondered what was happening. We felt that God wanted us in Lesotho. It was only a two to four year term. Now they were telling us the door to Lesotho was closed? How could this be? God is the God of order. What did He want us to do? We prayed and praised Him and waited before Him for further direction.

We did not feel led to go to Montreal. We finally called M.C.C. and told them we did not feel we were to go to Montreal and we still felt God was speaking to us about Lesotho. Despite this, the M.C.C. people encouraged us to pursue the opportunity in Montreal. They even scheduled a weekend visit to the church there. However, after much prayer and discussion we clearly knew that we were not to go there. We told the mission office and from their point of view, it looked like we would be staying home.

We continued our work at the church. We had been working with troubled youth and were seeing good results.

About six weeks later, Betty called me. The mission had phoned and asked us how soon we could go to Lesotho. She said they needed an answer by the end of the week.

I told her, "When God speaks to me, we'll go, and not before then."

I earnestly sought the Lord about this. I was happy where I was. Life was good. Surely, God had not given me this new job for nothing! But as I prayed, I felt God asking me, "Charles, I gave you this new job that you've wanted for so long. Are you willing to give it up to serve Me?"

From then on it was clear to me. It was November. M.C.C. called and Betty handed me the phone. They asked, "Can you be at orientation in Akron, Pennsylvania on January 10?"

To Betty's surprise, I said, "Yes."

So we packed up our belongings, stored our furniture in the basement, leased the rest of the house, and visited our families for Christmas. We didn't come back to the house until six years later for a three-month leave. After many farewells and good-byes, not without tears, we were off to missionary orientation.

At missionary orientation, we were the only couple with children. We were also older than most of the other people. And, of course, we were the only mixed race family there.

One day in the cafeteria at lunch, a young lady came and sat beside us. She seemed to wear a perpetual smile.

She introduced herself, "My name is Nina."

I extended my hand, "I'm Charles, and this is my wife, Betty."

She immediately started a conversation with us, going on about this and that. At one point she blurted out, "I just can't believe I'm sitting here opposite a black and white couple. I'll have to write my parents about this. They'll never believe it. And you're missionaries, too! Like, WOW!"

At that, Betty and I could no longer contain ourselves. We looked at each other and burst into laughter. Nina, sensing the humor, herself, joined us as we all laughed until it hurt.

In the mornings, we discussed culture shock, and how to work through it. They expected it to hit pretty hard. The afternoons were devoted to exercises and games to help us better relate to people. One of the exercises was a dependency game. We were teamed up two by two, but not with your spouse. One person was blindfolded. The other person led. The first half hour was difficult. Eventually, the leader would become more adept at explaining and preparing, while the blindfolded person developed more trust. It was an effective lesson. Overseas, you would be going to learn from the people. Then you could understand how to effectively reach and teach them.

However, we felt that the orientation was missing some critical elements. We had expected to spend more time in the Word, and in prayer, seeking to hear from God. When we brought this up to the leaders, they suggested that we open each session with prayer and Bible reading. So, we eagerly complied.

After orientation was over, we boarded the plane for Lesotho. With all of the stops, layovers, and changes, it took two full days of travel to get there. Finally we were on the plane flying over South Africa, approaching Johannesburg. It was January of 1979, the middle of their summer.

As we flew over the countryside approaching Johannesburg, we looked out the window to see a country made up of rolling hills and mountains. We couldn't tell Lesotho from South Africa as we flew over, but we could see that the land was indeed beautiful, but rugged.

From the air, the city of Johannesburg was impressive. It looked as if everyone had a swimming pool. The houses were big. It was a clean, well-organized city. This was where the white people lived. It looked pretty much like the area we had left in Canada. We didn't even recognize the homeland area where the black Africans lived as we flew over it.

I did have my apprehensions, though. The mission warned us that they didn't know what would happen to us during our two-day layover in Johannesburg. Because flights only went to Lesotho two times a week, we had to stay in an airport hotel for two nights. We knew about Apartheid and that we probably couldn't leave the hotel.

After the plane landed, we entered a fairly large and modern airport. This place was much like any airport in the United States, but smaller. All of the modern conveniences were in place. We noticed that menial work such as baggage handling and cleaning was done by black Africans while ticket sales and customer service jobs were performed strictly by white people.

When we arrived at the hotel, we were surprised to find that we were booked into a three star hotel. We expected a lower standard in Africa, but the hotel compared with any nice hotel in America. The staff booked us two rooms opposite each other. We wondered what we needed two rooms for. But, everything was paid for. So, we spent our days in one room, and our nights in the other. The rooms were attractive and well-furnished, but the windows were secured and there was a wall around the hotel. You couldn't see anything of the outside world. It was a lush prison.

The hotel staff was very friendly. The black employees would watch us in obvious surprise. The white staff was a little more discreet. Barry, who was five-years-old at the time and Tina, who was four, seemed to be oblivious to all of the stares around them. With their childlike charm they quickly made friends with most of the staff. We had excellent service. At one point, the waiter offered us coffee; even Tina, who said, "Yes, please," very prim and proper. After adding cream and sugar, we watched her as she tried a sip. "Bitta, bitta, bitta," and a puckered face was her response. Even the waiter laughed.

Chapter 11

AFRICA

Out of Johannesburg we flew on a twenty-passenger Twin Otter turboprop plane to Maseru, the capitol city of Lesotho. The plane was built in Canada and designed for a short approach and takeoff. It also handled well on less than perfect landing strips–even on dirt or gravel. The Maseru airport was quite a contrast from Johannesburg International. It did not have the modern gates, or many of the modern conveniences, as did the Johannesburg airport.

As we disembarked from the plane down the portable staircase onto the tarmac, we were greeted by many of our fellow missionaries. One after another they introduced themselves and made us feel very welcome. We were surprised to discover that everyone who met us at the airport was from a mission organization. As we conversed with our newfound friends, we realized how much there was to learn. But then, again, that was part of our mission; to learn.

Our M.C.C. directors intentionally drove us first through the worst area of the city. We saw people living in small mud huts with grass or thatched roofs or corrugated tin held down by concrete blocks. Kids were running around naked and filthy. People sat in dust and dirt and cooked on open fires. It was clearly a poverty stricken area.

When we got inside the city, the differences between South Africa and Lesotho were even more apparent. The roads were all dirt or gravel. The "three star hotel" in Maseru was nothing like the hotel we had just left in Johannesburg.

We first went to the home of our M.C.C. directors for tea. After tea, they escorted us to our temporary quarters called the "arrival center." The arrival center consisted of a number of tiny dwellings built by the government. They were pre-fab houses made of wall-board and covered with tin roofs. They didn't have foundations, but sat on pilings–not very sturdy. In the bathrooms where the pipes left the room, you could look out to ground underneath. There were Dutch doors at the front and back. Generally, the top part was left open for ventilation during the day. Each house had three bedrooms, a bathroom, and a kitchen/living area combination with running water and electricity. The bedrooms were so minute that the double beds took up nearly all of the room. There was just a small walkway around them. There were quite a few people staying at the arrival center, mostly Africans from other countries moving into Lesotho. We would stay there for about ten days while our permanent quarters were being built.

Our new friends took us to the M.C.C. main house where the rest of the missionaries welcomed us with a dinner of spinach lasagna, garlic bread, salad, and a delicious tea called Rooibos.

After dinner we went to our temporary home in the arrival center. In the kitchen were all the utensils and cutlery that we needed. There were two tea towels and four bath towels for our use. Everything was inventoried before and after we left to be sure we did not pilfer anything. To make us feel more "normal," on one of our first days, Betty used a pop bottle to roll out a crust and made an apple pie.

For the next several days we were just allowed to experience Maseru, and Lesotho in general. Our jobs did not start for a few days. So we walked into town.

The natural beauty of Lesotho struck us immediately. The skies were deep blue, and usually very clear. The air was crisp and clean. The sun was bright and hot. Although the latitude of the area was similar to that of Houston, Texas, the sun could be a hazard. Because of the altitude the air was thinner, and there was less atmosphere to filter out the ultra-violet rays. We took a short walk uptown and Betty received a severe sunburn so she had to wear a hat from then on. When it rained, it came down in torrents–often an inch or more–but immediately afterwards the sun would come out and shine brightly. Ten minutes later the dust was blowing again. The only evidence of the downpour was the puddles and washed out roads.

The sunsets were truly magnificent; especially in our temporary home! As the sun dipped into the mountains the sky around it became painted in a glorious fashion with oranges, pinks, purples, and blues. The stars at night seemed close enough to touch. They were right on top of us. At the end of a hard day we would love to sit outside in the dark, just watching the stars, praising God for this special gift of His handiwork to us.

We were a curiosity to the Basotho people, who were very friendly. Most everyone we saw wanted to feel our children's hair. This frightened Barry and Tina at first, but they soon became accustomed to it. Most of the Basotho wore brightly colored woolen blankets and straw hats. When going into Maseru, the crowded streets of people clad in these blankets created a kaleidoscope of color.

Many of the Basotho used horses for transport, while a few drove cars. However, most people walked barefoot wherever they wanted to go. They frequently carried their shoes and donned them when they arrived at their destination. Although we had been told that English was the second language of the Basotho, we found that most people could not speak it and didn't understand the English that *we* spoke. They could only use a few broken phrases. One of their favorites was "hello mommy" or "hello daddy." Being black, they expected me to speak Sesotho. I had several conversations with them where they couldn't understand why I didn't. I informed them that Africa is a big place with many languages. They still didn't understand what I was talking about.

During our first week in Lesotho, our M.C.C. directors took us into downtown Maseru to a local café, just to see what it was like. The streets were bustling with people, and the sidewalks were extremely crowded. As we left the café, a group of young men bumped into us. I felt a hand go into my pocket. I grabbed the hand and walked on several steps, keeping a wide-eyed youth in my grasp. Finally, when I released the hand, the now frightened young man disappeared into the crowd. We were told that pickpockets were very common downtown, and that they usually targeted people new to the area.

Our directors suggested that I wear a money belt, and never carry a wallet in my back pocket. We were told that the women put their money in their dairy; their bras. You could see a woman walking down the street with the outline of her coins showing through. There was a lot to learn in those early days.

Although most of the homes in Maseru were brick or concrete block, most of the houses in the villages were made of sticks and poles and reeds. These were held together with a dung and mud mixture, then rocks, piled one on top of the other. They used the same dung and mud mixture as a mortar to stabilize the whole structure. The floors were of dirt. Each year the women would smear the houses with a thin mixture of dung and mud.

After the mixture dried, it always gave the house a freshly painted appearance. Some of the people would even use fancy designs to decorate their homes. Sheets of iron or tin anchored at the corners with concrete blocks were often used for the roofs. Many of the houses had a grass roof made of thatch. Thatch was usually a better roof because of its insulating qualities. It was always cooler in the summer and warmer in the winter than the iron roofs. But in extremely rainy times, these huts would collapse and just melt away. They would generally last two to four years.

The people made good use of what they had. The children would use the dung mixture to create animal sculptures. They would also create intricate vehicles out of wire and tin and flattened pop or beer cans. One particularly striking sculpture was an ostrich riding a bicycle. The women were always making mats and hats, and would work with beads. They would sell these as souvenirs beside the road.

Many of the homes were called rondovals. A rondoval was a round structure with a thatched roof that came to a point. Usually spacious on the inside, it was warm in the winter and cool in the summer. They had only one room.

After ten days in the arrival center, we were finally placed in our permanent housing. It was in an area called Lithabaneng (pronounced dee-thab-a-ning), about six kilometers or four and a half miles from the capital city of Maseru. Because I was actually a government employee, the Lesotho government built this house especially for us. We were the only foreigners living in the area.

Our house was a simple rectangular concrete block house with an iron roof. It was a no frills house. The floor had something similar to black tarpaper covering the concrete. The walls were painted black about halfway up, with the upper part white. Betty had a fit. She said, "This has got to change!" The builder was an American. We had a good relationship right away. He had the walls repainted a soft creamy eggshell for us and I put down stick-on carpeting squares for flooring. The M.C.C. paid for half. The M.C.C. also gave us furniture from people who left after their three-year term with the mission.

One of the pieces was a huge wardrobe–about as big as one of our rooms. The government supplied a farm tractor and trailer to help us move our furniture. We could only get a few pieces on at a time. We were also driving on gully-washed roads and had to move very slowly. We began to learn about African time; nothing is done in a hurry.

There were two bedrooms, one of which Barry and Tina shared with bunk beds while Betty and I occupied the other. We had a living room with a kitchen table at one end. There was a small kitchen, with only a sink, no cupboards of any kind. I made some shelves upon which to store dishes and food. We also had a small bathroom. A twenty-gallon solar heater, which did not hold the heat very long after the sun went down, supplied hot water to the bathtub. It didn't take us long to learn to bathe before sunset if we wanted hot water. The bathtub had been installed with the drain end higher than the other end. Every time we took a bath we had to battle to push the water out the drain.

The only electricity was a forty-watt light bulb in each room. We could only have four of the five on at one time. Otherwise, we would overload the circuit and trip the breaker. For cooking we had a gas stove, with the gas bottle sitting right next to the stove. There was also a paraffin (kerosene) refrigerator. It served its purpose, but every couple of weeks it would belch out a blue-black smoke that would cover everything in the house with a fine black dust. You had to trim the wick periodically. It was a far cry from what we had left in Canada, but it was our home and we loved it.

Betty's favorite part of our home was the rondoval. It was a separate structure located about twenty steps outside our kitchen. I had to agree, it was lovely. Connected to the house by a brick patio, we put a sofa, table, and chairs in it and spent most of our time there. We used lamps and a gas heater in the winter. The rondoval was cooler in the summer and warmer in the winter. We were home!

During that time, both Betty and I started our jobs. Betty was an administrative assistant in the M.C.C. office in Maseru. I began my job with the government training mechanics. My job was an unusual foray for the M.C.C.. The government had gone to them for help. They wanted a man of integrity and hoped they would find that in a Christian volunteer.

For many weeks, although I showed up for work, there was nothing to do. My superiors asked that I arrive in January, but there was no structure in place. I did have an office and I went on a couple of repair missions, traveling in a Land Rover for hours and hours on bumpy rutted dirt roads, being bounced all over. I ached for days afterwards. There was always a driver, because these projects were in remote areas and the roads were vague.

I was working mainly with conservation projects in the mountains–building dams or lakes. Sometimes it was just terracing for farmland. You just had to know where you were going. They used no bulldozers or earthmovers, just tractors with scoops; thirty to forty of them. The projects took years. But, what were years in this country? The other thing I found strange and frustrating was the lack of books. I expected at least some manuals, but there were none. Overall, in my four years with the government, I felt I really had accomplished very little as far as training tractor mechanics. Most of the people I had to work with had basically no concept of an engine and I had to spend more of my time repairing the engines that were there. I did use the time productively to study the language and the people.

Chapter 12

HA SEFAKO

Our new neighbors were wonderful. Although at first we could not understand them, nor could they understand us, they brought us gifts. One neighbor brought us a rooster and a chicken. I built a pen for them in the back of the house along with a little shelter for their protection. Barry and Tina named them Mr. and Mrs. Chug-a-lug. The hen soon had baby chicks. They grew and kept us supplied in eggs for many years.

Another neighbor brought Barry and Tina each a puppy of their very own. One was light tan colored with black spots. The other one was a black longhaired dog with white paws. They both loved to play with the children. We named them Theodore and Alvin. I built a concrete and mud doghouse with a tin roof, right outside the kitchen door. Unfortunately both of them were hit and killed by cars within a short time. About six weeks later the same neighbor gave Barry and Tina a tan colored puppy. It was a mutt, but looked like a Labrador. This time, I built a fenced area where "Sandy" lived for many happy years.

Another neighbor brought us four big ears of corn. Betty had always loved corn on the cob, so this looked as though it was going to be a treat. However, it didn't look like the corn we had eaten in America. It was white, with small kernels. The kernels were hard, like the horse corn that we grow in America. Betty dutifully put a pot of water on to boil, put salt in it, and put the four ears of corn in. It didn't look as though it was softening, so she continued to boil it for over an hour. When we took the corn out, it was as hard as when we had started. Much later Betty learned that the best way to prepare the corn was to roast it over an open fire and then peel off one kernel at a time. It still took lots of chewing, but we eventually grew quite fond of it. We found that many people would take a roasted cob to work with them for their noon meal.

We also learned that when the Basotho bring you gifts, it's more hospitable to offer to prepare whatever they bring and ask them to eat it with you, or share it with them.

The water spigot for the village was just across from our house. Early one morning, I heard voices at the spigot. Women had lined up to get their water for the day. Even young women would hoist and carry 25 gallon buckets. The water would slosh around and they would move their heads along with the movement of the water to balance it. This particular morning, as I looked, I couldn't believe my eyes. A very attractive, fully developed teenager had joined the group and she wore only a skirt! Immediately, I called out to Betty, "You must come now! You won't believe this!" Later, we learned that many young women in the villages didn't really cover themselves until after initiation school. While driving to a village on several different occasions, we saw six or eight young ladies with their bodies smeared with some sort of white substance running beside the road. When we asked about it we were told we must not look or even notice, and it is never talked about because those girls were attending initiation school.

In front of our Rondoval, we started a vegetable garden consisting of onions, lettuce, broccoli, carrots, and tomatoes. Because of the dry climate and poor soil, it took a lot of effort. Each year we were sure to fertilize the ground. It became routine for Barry and me to make the trip to a local chicken farm to get chicken manure for the garden. We would dutifully spread the manure on the garden to make it grow. Of course watering was a must. Lesotho's climate was pretty dry, and the occasional thunderstorm did not do enough to keep the soil moist for growing. We always put a black shade over the garden because the noonday sun was too hot. Although we were definitely amateur gardeners, our neighbors were amazed at how we could get that garden to grow.

There were no vacuum cleaners, no televisions, no dishwashers, and no washing machines. We did get a lady to help with the laundry. Otherwise we did most of our work ourselves. Some of the local ladies made brooms that they sold in the market. They were about two feet long, made of grass tied together about two inches thick and surprisingly effective at lifting and moving dirt.

During the summertime, (December through February) it was daylight until about 8:30 in the evening. Most people went to bed after dark. It didn't take long for us to fall into that habit. At night, the light was too dim for any reading and our electric supply was sporadic at best. It took lots of candles and much lantern oil if you stayed up past dark.

In the early evenings, we would take walks in the neighborhood and get to know our neighbors better. Sometimes we would take bike rides as a family throughout the village area. We loved our family time. The lack of television or other forms of entertainment became a blessing for us and we grew close because we did so many things together.

Relationships were precious and we did not take them for granted. Another couple, Steve and Linda, had children opposite of ours. Their girl was Barry's age and their boy was Tina's age. Although we were from two different organizations, we seemed to connect with them from the very beginning. We were with the M.C.C. while they were with the African Inland Mennonite Mission (AIMM). The focus of the two groups was somewhat different. The M.C.C. consisted mainly of short-term, volunteer, career people who ministered to people through practical and vocational means. For example, my job was helping to train men in mechanics and tractor repair. We had not really chosen this road, but it had chosen us. It was an inroad to the mission field.

On the other hand, Steve was a missionary working with independent churches in the mountains. He spoke Sesotho fluently and truly had a heart for the people of the area. So he worked more closely with the people on a spiritual basis. Linda taught at Maseru prep school. We would have meals together and do puzzles. As we became closer, we seemed to complement each other.

We wanted to learn Sesotho but the people always wanted us to speak English so they could learn English. Even during down times at work, the men would sit with me and we'd go over English grammar. So many words challenged them with their use, like the word 'read' with its different pronunciations and usages.

Having a car became an issue. The M.C.C. had made a decision that missionaries would not have a car. Betty was appalled. Barry and Tina's school was in Maseru, about eight kilometers away. To get the children to school at eight would have meant leaving the house at 5 a.m. in a taxi. Taxis filled up quickly during commuting time. Some people got up at 3 a.m. just to get a seat in a taxi.

So, I decided to buy a car. However, when I told them, the directors would not allow it. I reminded them that they had made a promise to supply everything we needed. So, the M.C.C. made use of the fact that I was a good mechanic. We were assigned a parade of cars with one different defect or another. There would be stretches where we would have a different car every day. We drove a Peugeot, an Opel, and a Volkswagen Beetle–just to name a few.

One of the most interesting vehicles we drove was the Nomad. This vehicle was manufactured in South Africa. It was like a little old army Jeep; a high square looking vehicle, with just the basics, i.e. seats, a steering wheel, and an engine. It may have had springs and shock absorbers, but it didn't seem like it. When we hit a pothole we felt as though it would knock the fillings out of our teeth. It was so loud that we had to shout to carry on a conversation.

Even with our car, the morning commute to school still took over an hour. Although the distance was short, the trip was long, due to perpetual stop-and-go, bumper-to-bumper traffic. In order to get the kids to school on time, we would leave the house at about seven o'clock to arrive by eight. Many of our neighbors would come running to catch a lift with us as well. We were always loaded to capacity. Since we went right by my shop, Betty would drop me off first. She wouldn't even pull in. I'd just jump out in traffic.

Often there would be a knock at the door in the middle of the night. Someone was sick and needed to go to the hospital, or someone was having a baby and needed a doctor immediately. We learned to always keep the car full of gas, ready to go at a moment's notice to help our new neighbors.

One evening we went into town to see the movie, "The Sound of Music," being shown at Barry and Tina's school hall in Maseru. There were over one hundred fifty people packed into that little hall, all sitting on hard benches, all trying to see the movie. The body heat generated by everyone there combined with the humidity made it almost unbearable. Although the movie was wonderful, all Betty and I could think was, "Will this ever end?"

Near the end of the movie, as the Trapp family escaped the Nazis into the mountains, the wind outside began to blow fiercely. Suddenly, lightning flashed followed almost immediately by a huge clap of thunder, then total darkness. All power was off.

Instinctively we groped for our children. Each lightning flash illuminated the room for a split second. With each flash I caught a glimpse, first of Tina, then Barry. Taking their hands and staying close, we made our way out of the hall. We raced to our car, trying to beat the storm. Alas, it was not to be.

When we were about fifty feet from our car, the skies opened up with a downpour. We felt as if we were running under Niagara Falls, the storm was so intense. After we piled into the car, I started it and we headed for home. The windshield wipers on our car tried desperately to keep up, but visibility was zero. I had never seen a storm such as this. The lightning lit up the sky every few seconds, followed by huge claps of thunder, then total darkness with rain pouring down around us in torrents. When we finally arrived at the dirt road to our house we were shocked to see not a road, but a river leading to our home.

I said, "Betty, I'm not sure whether the road is here or if it's been washed away. I'll walk in front of the car and you drive."

"Charles?"

"It's okay honey. I'll be all right."

With a worried look, Betty slid behind the wheel.

I walked slowly in front of the car, trying to feel the road with my feet and water swirling around my knees. What normally took us five minutes took over a half hour. By the time we came to our compound gate, I was soaking wet and exhausted. When we finally opened our door, we were shocked to see about two feet of water in our home. While Betty and I gasped, Barry and Tina seized the opportunity to swim and splash in the water. Everything was an adventure to them. They felt no fear or tension. As Betty and I desperately fought the water, the children giggled with glee at their new indoor "swimming pool." The storm stopped just as suddenly as it had begun.

While the children splashed and frolicked in the water, Betty and I set to the task of sweeping the water out of the house. Barry and Tina became a little nervous when they noticed little black crabs swimming in the water with them. After we assured them the crabs wouldn't hurt them, the kids cautiously began to play with the crabs.

The next day, I went out in the yard early, grading the land to direct water away from the house. We were never flooded again.

One night we were sharing our visions and passions with Steve and Linda. They saw and knew, as we did, that we were not called to Lesotho to fix tractors, but to win souls for Jesus. One night as we talked together, Linda interjected, "You have to meet this couple we know who are in Ha Sefako. I know you will love them and you and they have lots in common. They'll be here next week."

We suggested that they bring their friends over and have dinner with us.

A week later, Steve and Linda brought their friends, John and Patty, over to meet us. They had four, very rambunctious children, from the ages of two years to seven years old. We noticed that this couple was amazingly full of peace. We all had such a wonderful time of fellowship together. We were just amazed. They obviously had something that we wanted and needed.

Betty, in her typical forthright fashion, asked, "What is it that makes you guys so different?"

They both just smiled at us.

That night they insisted that we come to visit them for a weekend in Ha Sefako, way up in the mountains. Of course we agreed. About three weeks later, right after I got home from work at 1:00 p.m., we piled into the car and headed to Ha Sefako.

This was the first time we had ventured out of the Maseru-Lithabaneng area on our own. After traveling for about an hour we found ourselves on little dirt roads or trails. There were no signs, so we couldn't really tell if we were on a road or not. Also about this time, I noticed that the engine was running a little hot. I stopped the car and looked under the hood. I found that the thermostat was no longer working, so the car was getting too hot.

We had to stop and add water to the radiator. From that point on, we stopped at every stream to replenish the radiator.

When the drive began to exceed the four or five hours we planned on, the sun dropped low into the sky and we knew it would be dark soon. Almost immediately, the stars began to appear, and we knew we were in trouble. Would we be lost out here? Surely not! We had been warned on many occasions by other missionaries that we must never be caught out after dark in an area we didn't know. We began to pray and recite the verse from Proverbs, "Trust in the Lord with all your hearts, and lean not unto your own understanding."

There was no light at all and it was absolutely pitch dark. I decided to stop the car at the side of the road and we would spend the night in the car. We did not want to take the chance of driving into a ravine or straying so far from the road that we would not find our way back or drive far from our route. There was also the danger of running into a house or village.

Shortly after we stopped, we were startled when three people emerged out of the darkness and appeared at the side of our car. Fortunately, one of the men spoke English. He invited us to sleep in the village because it was too dangerous to stay in the car. I told him where we were headed and who we were looking for. He knew the area, and he knew John and Patty. He exclaimed, "You are here! You are here! Come, I show you."

I knew that "here" could mean another 10 kilometers, so I said, "Come, get in the car."

So the man climbed into the car with us and guided us to John and Patty's home.

I was right. It was almost forty-five minutes before we got to our destination. We were learning when the Basotho say it's right here, be prepared for another journey. When we got to John and Patty's driveway, it went almost straight up and it was a lane-way (trail) combination of dirt and gravel. It was so dark, we could only see right in front of us and we had no idea what lay ahead at the top of the hill so we had to be very cautious. The car ran out of power. Our guide and the kids got out of the car to lighten it up. We had to inch our way up in first gear and it took a half an hour.

When we finally arrived we heard a child's voice say, "Mum, Dad, there's someone here!"

In an instant we were greeted by our new friends and their four rambunctious kids. One child grabbed our bags while the others hurried Barry and Tina into their house.

John and Patty came and embraced us asking, "Where have you been? Did you have trouble along the way?"

"Well, a little, but we made it." I replied.

We turned to thank the man that had brought us to our destination, only to find that he was already gone. We were really praising God for providing for us so perfectly.

We ate and fellowshipped together and fell into bed exhausted.

The next morning we arose to a good hot breakfast. All of the children were up. They had three boys and one girl, all of whom seemed to be in perpetual motion. They stopped only for the prayer before the meal. It didn't take Barry and Tina long to join in the fun. Meanwhile, John and Patty seemed oblivious to the noise.

After breakfast, John and I went outside to do a few chores. Betty helped Patty with the dishes. When we got back to the house, Patty gave us a book and a tape about the power of the Holy Spirit. The tape was by an Anglican Priest who shared in his sermon how his church had spiritually exploded when he received the baptism of the Holy Spirit. We thanked them and said that we would read the book and listen to the tape.

We worked, played and laughed together for the rest of the weekend. That weekend was the beginning of a lasting friendship.

On Sunday, after a wonderful and uplifting church service, we returned home. As I drove, Betty read the book out loud most of the trip home. As the sun began to set, we were comforted by the lights of Lithabaneng in the distance. Before we went to bed, we listened to the tape. Humbled by what the priest had to say, we knelt next to our bed and began to pray. We asked God to fill us to overflowing with the power of the Holy Spirit and with the evidence of speaking in tongues. Within moments we found ourselves praying in tongues.

The next evening, Betty told me that she had spoken to some of our new missionary friends about our experience with the Holy Spirit and praying in tongues. She was surprised by their reaction. We tried telling some others about it, with the same results. Most of them did not think this experience was of God. One person even told us we were dabbling in things from the evil one. We were troubled by this and decided to be still and say nothing more. But, we were confused by their words and behavior, because we all read the same Bible. What else could it mean in Mark 16:17, when it reads "And these signs shall follow them that believe...they shall speak with new tongues" or in Jude 20, when it says, "But ye, beloved, building up yourselves on your most holy faith, praying in the Holy Ghost"?

As we continued to study God's Word we were learning through these scriptures, and many others, that praying in tongues was one of the best ways to stimulate our faith and help us learn to trust God more easily and more completely. God was blessing us and we felt as though we were bubbling over with His love.

I could feel the strength of His love at this very moment and I felt no fear. I had no concerns about my personal safety. The blessing of being able to speak to God with words when there were no words was a real comfort to me. I focused on the problem at hand; finding a way out.

Chapter 13

LET HER GO

The phone rang and I hurried to pick it up. I thought it must be Charles calling back. Instead, my brother's voice came through. "Betty, have you heard from Charles?"

"Yes," I answered, "and he is fine."

My brother said, "I'm sure this has changed your plans to go back. Why don't you come and stay with us now?"

"I can't possibly do that." I replied. "We have to go back."

Furiously, he said, "All I can say to you is that you are a fool."

I explained to him that I couldn't possibly think of leaving Charles alone there.

I understood how my family felt. They were worried about our safety. This was not the first time that people thought we were fools when it came to our serving in Africa.

My mind drifted back to the time when we were first thinking of going to Lesotho, Tina's health issues were

serious enough that they would have stopped most people from going.

In the years before we left for Lesotho, Tina had been hospitalized many times with severe asthma attacks. Several times, I thought she was going to die in my arms. As a result, we took great precautions with our house to keep her healthy. We air-conditioned our home, and put air purifiers by her bed. After we made the decision to go to Lesotho, we consulted our doctor about Tina's asthma condition.

Surprisingly, he suggested that since Lesotho was a very arid country, she would probably be much healthier there. The doctor's advice was heartening. We knew that God was leading us and He would take care of us.

We found it true that it was very hot, dry and dusty in Lesotho. Tina's asthma was no problem for the first three months. Then one day our neighbors brought a herd of sheep and penned them in just outside our bedroom window. The houses were close together, so no matter what one neighbor did, the others shared. It was just a part of life that everyone took for granted.

At two in the morning Charles shook me gently. "Betty, something's wrong with Tina."

With those words I awoke immediately and went straight to her room. We found her in labored breathing, struggling for every breath.

I picked her up and held her in my arms. We prayed for her healing.

Charles looked at me. "Betty, I'll get the car started and you pack up some things for her. She needs to go to the hospital. Wake Barry!"

"All right, let's take her to Roma." A friend of ours from the mission was a nurse at Roma. She had told us to come there if we had any needs.

So all four of us piled into the car and headed to Roma. It was about forty kilometers away. Charles and Barry sat in the front, while I sat in the back with Tina, holding her and praying all the way.

When we arrived at the hospital, the doctors there had no idea how to treat her. They put her in a croup vapor tent and she continued to struggle for every breath. Finally, after ten days, we brought her home, still very sick and very weak. We saw no improvement in her condition. We continued to pray and a day or two later she began to breathe easier. We were rejoicing.

The very next Sunday, we were introduced to a doctor from Uganda. We found he was practicing at the hospital in Maseru. When we told him about Tina's asthma attack, he invited us to his home so he could examine her.

A few weeks later Tina experienced another severe attack. Again, she could not breathe. This time we took her into Maseru to the Ugandan doctor. He put her in the QEII hospital in Maseru, and started an IV of cortisone. He emphasized to us that she was really fighting for her life. Charles took Barry back home to get some rest and I stayed with Tina.

I kept vigil next to Tina. I prayed fervently as I watched her struggle so hard for every breath. I cried out to God, "Lord, You brought us here. We have much work to do here. I can't watch Tina go through this. You can heal her! I know you can!" With that prayer I began to sob softly.

Tina's eyes were closed as she continued to labor for breath. I could see by the monitor that her pulse was racing, struggling for oxygen to supply her little body. Now the fear rising in my soul seemed to be choking me as well, taking my own breath away. I felt desperate.

Suddenly a peace settled over me as I heard a voice within my spirit saying, "I know how much you love her. She is mine. Let her go."

"Let her go?" I thought. "What does that mean? Will she die? No, I can't! I love her so much."

I knew that I had to pray and worship God. For an hour I sat there, praying for His mercy. I struggled with the idea of letting her go. Did God mean that we would lose our child, the way so many other parents had lost children? As her mother I felt I could not let go. She was a special 'gift from God' to me.

Then, as I was praying, I remembered how God had asked Abraham for his only son, Isaac, to be offered as a sacrifice. How must Abraham have felt, not only losing his only son with very little prospect of having another, but having to take him by his own hand? Yet he was faithful. He went to the point of raising the knife to offer Isaac as a sacrifice before God himself stopped him.

God had not asked me to take my own child's life, but He wanted me to put her totally into His hands. Could I trust God that much? Suppose He wanted to take her back to Himself. I could not bear the thought.

As I thought of Abraham, I remembered how God had spared Isaac. I hoped that God would do the same for me.

As I wept and prayed, a peace came over me. I began to realize that no matter what, God wanted me to trust Him, to really trust Him. I put Tina in God's hands. And as I did, the peace of God flooded my being. I just knew that everything would be all right. God established Himself as the total Lord over my life, and all that was dear to me. I was beginning to see that I could trust Him completely, in every area, with everything.

In my heart I knew that God was faithful to hear and answer our prayers. I continued to plead for Tina's healing.

As I prayed, Charles walked in. I took his hand, looked into his eyes and through my tears I said, "Oh, honey, I was praying for her, and a voice within my spirit said that we must trust God and let her go."

He looked at me and said, "I wanted to come and share with you. As I've been praying, I too, have felt God saying that we must give her to Him and trust Him completely."

We held each other close and prayed, "Father God, both of our children are a special gift from You. Now, right now, we give them back to you. We know that you love our children even more than we do. Thank you, Father. In Jesus' Name we pray. Amen!"

About six hours later, Tina was still struggling to breathe, with an I.V. in her arm. The doctor came in for rounds, examined her, and said, "She seems to be getting a bit stronger."

Then he turned to us and said, "We must be very careful in the future. She may not survive another asthma attack. We must do everything we can to keep her from having another attack."

As the days passed, we watched her slowly getting stronger. Finally, she was well enough to complain about the crib. It had a very rough straw mattress and it was a little small for her. She had to lie on her side to fit in it. Within a week, we took her home.

One of the first people to welcome us home was a neighbor who brought a live chicken and put it in Tina's hands. As Tina tried to hold it, it flapped its wings wildly sending feathers everywhere. I must admit, I thought, 'Oh no, chicken feathers!'

But, nothing happened. She had no reaction at all.

Soon, many people arrived to give Tina their best wishes. They were so glad she was out of the hospital and home again.

Later that afternoon Ntate Mohono, an Independent Church pastor, knocked at our door. We had met him previously at our mission's office and we were very fond of him and his wife.

Charles invited him in. He was a very tall man, over six feet. Most Basotho men are about five feet tall.

After spending some time in our greetings, Ntate Mohono said, "I am concerned for the health of your child; I hear that she has been very sick."

Charles replied, "Yes, she has been very sick, but she seems to be getting better."

"But what of your future plans in our country? If she is not healed, will you be willing to stay with us?"

Charles and I exchanged looks, not knowing how to answer that question.

Ntate continued, "We do not want you to leave. The Lord brought you to us and I pray that He does not take you away because of your child. May I pray over her, for her healing?"

"Of course you may."

So Ntate Mahono began to pray. As he prayed, he continually referred to Tina as 'him'. He asked that God would heal him and grant him a long healthy life and grant us all a long stay in Lesotho. The referral to Tina as 'him' didn't bother us because we knew that our Lord understood.

The next morning we were about to give Tina her cortisone tablet and she asked, "If Jesus healed me, why do I have to take this pill?"

I looked at her, then at Charles. We both asked, "Do you know that God has really healed you?"

She nodded vigorously in agreement.

"Then you don't need this pill?"

"No," Tina countered. "I am healed."

We then went together and flushed the pills down the toilet.

We continued to see the doctor for our regular visits to check on her condition. Each time he would comment, "We are seeing remarkable improvement. You see, the cortisone really is helping her. Her lungs are getting clearer with every visit."

After about the third visit we informed him that she had not taken the medication since the day she was released from the hospital.

He looked at us incredulously, "You have not been giving her the medicine I gave you?"

We both shook our heads.

"Well, this is a miracle because she is getting healthier every day."

Tina never had another asthma attack. Because of where we lived, there were animals around us constantly. They were just a part of life. But Tina did not react to them ever again. She later had her own horse and was a very good rider.

It became the prayer of our hearts and a very real truth to us that for the rest of our lives we would know that GOD IS MORE THAN ENOUGH. We offered our children unto Him with fear and trembling. Even in our reluctance, God showed Himself to be patient, loving, and kind. He continually showed us how very much he loves us.

Chapter 14

STARTING WITH CHILDREN

We had only been in Lesotho a few weeks, when our M.C.C. director said, "Betty, maybe you'd like to come with me to meet Joan." I decided to go with her, because I was keen to learn as much as I could in my new surroundings.

Joan was a South African white lady who chose to live in Lesotho. So I imagined she would be similar to the women I had seen in Johannesburg. Most of us lived and dressed rather informally. I usually wore sandals, with no stockings, t-shirts and wrap-around skirts with my long hair simply tied back. However, the white South African women usually dressed very well with their hair done up and always wearing elaborate makeup, jewelry and stockings.

Amazingly, Joan dressed like me! Upon walking into Joan's home, I was immediately impressed with her warmness, with her sincerity and with her obvious love for others and their needs. This was the beginning of a lasting friendship that was to become very meaningful to me.

Joan was very concerned about how best to help the women of Lesotho. Most of the women lived in Lesotho without their husbands, because most of their men worked in the South African mines. It was up to the women to work, care for the family and hold the home together. They often only saw their husbands twice a year, at Easter and at Christmas. Some husbands tried to come home every month, but because of poor transportation and the expense involved, many more stayed at the mines until the longer holidays.

Joan and I used to get together every week with several Basotho ladies. We enjoyed tea together and talked about the problems facing so many women in Lesotho. Not only were these women living separate from their husbands, some of them lived far from their children as well because of their jobs. It was really awesome to hear some of the stories these ladies had to share about hard times and hard work. We always closed our meetings with Bible readings and prayer.

Because we lived in an urban sprawl area, Joan thought we should hold our meetings at our house. I eagerly agreed. I invited our neighbors and we decided to change from a discussion group to a Bible study on the book of Isaiah because it was Joan's favorite book. We had ten ladies at our first meeting. Joan and I led jointly and found that we expressed ourselves very differently. She came from a Catholic background and I came from a Southern Baptist background. But, oh, how I grew to love the book of Isaiah and to appreciate and love my friend Joan more every day!

As I got to know Joan more every week, I found that she was always there for me. The more we met together the more I realized that I needed to do more where we lived. She and I prayed about it together and it came to me that I should start a play day for the children in the area, one day a week.

The first thing we had to do was get it approved through our mission organization. They were not too keen on the idea because it was not completely in line with their philosophy. They wanted not "to provide the people with fish, but to teach them how to fish." We agreed with them wholeheartedly in that philosophy, but to me there were too many children in our area that didn't seem to go to school. They seemed totally unmotivated and without hope. It disturbed me greatly. I felt that if we did no more than to create a vehicle that would give them an interest in life that it would be worth our while. The M.C.C. approved our project, but would not commit any resources to it. We would have to find our resources elsewhere.

Joan knew a lady whose father had established some of the early trading businesses in the area. She was very active in helping the people in Lesotho. If there was a big project for the benefit of the people, she was usually in the middle of it, frequently using her own resources to promote the project. She had access to food, clothing, and many of the necessities for ministering to the poor of the country.

So Joan and I, along with a couple of other white women from the area, drew up a plan for the play day and submitted it to this lady.

She looked over our proposal, and readily agreed to help us. She asked us how many children we expected to attend our play day. I suggested that we should have about fifty or so. She told us where to go to get powdered milk, flour, sugar, all kinds of baking supplies, clothing, and even some toys.

For weeks, we scurried to pick up the food supplies and toys. Some organizations also donated rolls and sheets of paper, which we needed to cut up. We recruited two more white ladies to help out. They agreed to bring their house help who were able to communicate better with the children in Sesotho, their own language. Joan brought her daughter to help us as well.

Our little house, already short on storage space, couldn't contain everything. Charles asked the men at the workshop if they could put up a small tool shed so we would have a place to store our supplies. They agreed to put it up. Unlike most of the buildings in the area, we needed a concrete floor to keep out the vermin and snakes. So, Charles and I poured the concrete, and it was up and ready to use within two days.

For the first play day we expected about fifty children. So on the Tuesday and Wednesday nights prior to that first day, Charles, Barry and Tina and I baked cookies. We tried to put everything in them that would be nutritious for the children. So we ended up with an oatmeal raisin cookie with walnuts and coconut. They were delicious! When we baked them, we made sure to make a huge cookie for each child, so they could each have a cookie and a glass of milk.

When that first Thursday arrived, sure enough we had about forty-five children. With that number we divided them by age groups so that they could all have exposure to each activity.

In Lesotho, many children do not really know their ages. So to divide them by age groups we gave them a test. They were to stand up straight and put their arm over the top of their head and try to touch their opposite ear. When a child was able to do this he was considered to be of school age. So we grouped them into "can't touch their ear yet" (pre-school), "could barely touch their ear" (early elementary), "could easily touch their ear" (middle elementary), and pre-teens to teens.

We planned four activities. The first one consisted of singing and games. In the second group we made musical instruments to make our own rhythm band. The third activity was arts and crafts. The other activity was reading Bible stories.

At first, we took so much for granted. And, when faced with the reality of the situation, we had to change our approach. We had to learn how to teach. For instance, when we asked the children to cut something out, it didn't occur to us that they would not know how to use scissors. So one day we had to just teach everyone how to use scissors. By the end of the session everyone was gleefully cutting shreds of paper. The next time they began to cut out different shapes. It wasn't long until most of them were able to cut out their body shapes that we made for them.

We were beginning to see first hand what a doctor in Morija had tried to explain to us. Many children were fed, bathed and taught daily chores. They were not allowed to ask questions or expect answers, or engage in any conversation with adults. In other words, they were simply neglected.

By far, the most popular activity became arts and crafts. We were always challenged to come up with new activities for this, but the children's enjoyment inspired us. On our first day, we used our huge rolls of paper. We had each child lie down on the sheet of paper while we traced an outline around his body. Then we had them make a face on the head, and color clothes on the picture to match what the child was wearing. If the child wore blue shorts, we colored them blue on the paper. After we finished we would put the child's name on the picture. All of them were so impressed by this idea. It became such a favorite that we had to do it several times a year.

Within a couple of weeks we had three hundred children attending our play day, every Thursday. Even in the winter, when it was very cold, we held our play day if the sun was shining. And, very seldom did it rain in the winter. We always worked with the children outside, because we had no indoors facility big enough. Usually, the sun would warm the area enough so that it was tolerable. We didn't serve cookies and cold milk during the cold days. Instead, we served a mug of soup and a huge piece of bread.

Throughout the duration of this entire project, we would occasionally go back to Joan's friend for supplies. She always found what we needed.

We continued this ministry as long as we were in Lithabaneng. Because the large number of children involved, it was always a large project. At first, the mothers of the children were shy about helping. They would just stand outside of the gate and watch. Finally, Me' Marjorie approached them about helping. It was, after all, for their children. After that, they became involved and took turns helping with the activities.

I'm not sure who enjoyed the play day more, the children, or us. We always did it together as a family and thoroughly enjoyed it. The children called me Me' Malerato, meaning Mother of Love. They called Tina Lerato (Love) and they called Barry Thabo (First Born). They called Charles Ntate Moruti (Pastor) or Morana (Big Chief).

I loved these people so much. How could I think of abandoning them? I knew we were going back to Lesotho.

Chapter 15

ADVENTURE

We had lived through several coup attempts. And, we had seen attacks on expatriates, usually targeting their businesses. These had been isolated events, and the firing usually stopped after a few hours. However, this time the violence was different. After the first few hours, around mid morning, thick black smoke started filling the air. Were people's homes on fire, or was it the downtown business district? I had never experienced so much burning. The smoke and the fighting kept growing more and more intense.

In a moment of calm, my thoughts ran wild. What would happen to the ministry if Betty didn't come back to Africa, or if I was evacuated never to return? Would our home be attacked? Would there even be a city left when this was over? Were our members alive? Where do we go from here? I didn't even have time to say goodbye to anyone.

I caught myself. This was not productive thinking. I shifted gears and trained my thoughts in a different direction.

My first assignment in Lesotho was to maintain a fleet of heavy equipment owned by the government for conservation projects. At the same, I was to train the workshop maintenance crew all the basics of mechanics, repairs and maintenance. These men had next to no exposure to machinery. Sometimes, people of influence in the government would bring their relatives into the program; and they were not necessarily qualified or even interested in pursuing a career in mechanics. They did not know the basic functions of engines, or what a transmission was, or why an engine needed oil. It was quite a challenge.

The tractors were located in different areas for various reasons. Often times a tractor would come into the shop needing an overhaul. An engine overhaul usually took several weeks. While the tractor was in for overhaul, it and its operator were both idle. The operator would live in the area above the shop, subsisting on mealy pop, a corn mash that was a common staple throughout Africa, and sleeping on his blanket until the tractor was fixed. Since I thought this was a phenomenal waste of manpower, I struck upon the idea of ordering two new Ford engines. They were pretty much interchangeable amongst most of the tractors in the fleet. So instead of having the tractor out of commission for five to six weeks, the operators could exchange the engines and have the tractor back into the field within a day or two. We would then take the old engine and rebuild it so it was ready for the next engine exchange.

The system worked well for a time, until someone higher up felt that having two whole engines in our parts warehouse was a waste, so they would not authorize parts to rebuild the old engines.

At other times I was required to go out and make repairs in the field. We would take parts and tools we thought we would need according to the assessment given by the operators in the field. Sometimes the assessments were better than others, but we were usually able to bring the right supplies based on what the operator told us was the problem.

The first time that I had to go into the field, I was accompanied by Abe. Abe was the works manager and he knew the location and was in essence the lead man on the job. We flew out early on Friday morning, because it was at least a full days' drive on rough dirt roads. We flew in the MAF Missions plane referred to as an islander or bush plane. I had a good idea of how long the job would take, so I assured Betty that I would be home late that night.

The plan was to fly to the site, make repairs on the two tractors, one of which required a new clutch and the other required some fuel injector cleaning, or possible replacement. We would then drive a water tank truck home. Many of the villages had no drinking water, so the government hauled portable water to them in large tanker trucks. The tanker would usually last for several weeks before needing to come back for replenishing. It sounded like a good, efficient plan.

Abe and I found the tractors just as expected. We replaced the new clutch and the fuel injectors. It was not a problem. We finished right on schedule, early in the afternoon.

Abe suggested, "Well, that's done. Let's get a good nights rest and leave early in the morning."

I had promised Betty I would be home, but a rest sounded good about now. As I wavered, Abe went on, "Let's have a little fun tonight."

I stared in stark unbelief. He winked at me, "Don't worry; you'll be glad we stayed."

About a half hour later he came back with a lady. "Charles, this is Irene, she is for you."

I just stared at him. "Look! I did not come up here to party and be unfaithful to my wife. You do what you want, but leave me out of it. Just make sure you're ready to leave early in the morning."

They laughed and left.

By this time I was angry and totally disgusted. I decided to try to get some rest. I knew I had no way to let Betty know that we were coming back later. I prayed for her and the kids and that God would give them peace.

At this hotel the electricity was created by diesel generators. The management usually turned off the generators at about 10:00 p.m. Then there was nothing but pitch dark.

Sometime during the night–I have no idea what time– Abe stumbled into the room we were sharing. He was profoundly drunk and flopped onto his bed where he stayed for the rest of the night. He fell asleep immediately then began snoring loudly. The alcohol fumes emanating from the man were very strong. He breathed loudly and heavily, and then, suddenly I didn't hear a thing. I began to feel concerned and wondered if Abe was dying. I thought, 'I have no idea how I can explain to the police why I have a dead man in my room.' Just then Abe began to breathe loudly again. I could not sleep the rest of the night.

The next morning Abe awoke, still in his clothes, with a headache and a hangover.

"Are you ready to go home now?" I asked.

"Just give me a little time. I'll be ready soon."

We went together and secured our tool boxes and spare parts chest to the tanker truck.

Abe mumbled something and then he disappeared. The next time I saw him was late that night, when he returned to the hotel drunk and disorientated. Now I was really irritated and angry with this irresponsible behavior. How long must I be stuck up here with no way back? I knew Betty must be getting concerned by now.

This time Abe came in a little earlier. After a few hours of sleep, we arose at 4:00 in the morning to leave for home. Since Abe was in no shape to drive, I took the first shift in driving the water tank truck home. As I drove, Abe gave the directions. By noon we were both extremely hungry. I wondered how or when we would eat because I saw nothing but a few scattered houses in this desolate land. Finally, we approached a village.

Abe said, "Let's stop here for something to eat."

I did as I was told, but I saw nothing to make me think we would be eating any time soon.

I parked the truck on the side of the road in the village. Abe approached a man and said something to him in Sesotho. The man beckoned both of us into a nearby cave where there was meat hanging in the cool shadows.

"It's lamb," Abe said. He chose two nice size pieces and paid the man. He then turned to me and said, "Come."

In every village there is usually a fire that is kept burning most of the time. On each fire there is always a pot that usually contains mealy-pop, which is similar to corn meal mush. So we went to the fire. There Abe found a shovel which was used to scoop the ashes out of the fire. He bought a few cents worth of salt, sprinkled it over the meat, placed the meat on the shovel and cooked the lamb over that open fire. When the meat was cooked, we paid a few cents for some mealy-pop and had a delicious lunch.

After lunch, we both felt better, Abe took over the driving. We knew that the trip would be long. It took us a little over fourteen hours to get home. It was a very long and very hard drive with the rough roads. My body ached all over for days after.

In Lithabaneng, Betty, Barry, and Tina were outside and ran to meet me as I came through the gate. As the sun was setting, I looked up our road to see our house, which looked very good to me right now. It was so good to be home.

We had a nice dinner together and put the children to bed.

Betty was anxious to know what had kept me.

I told her the whole story. She shared with me that it was hard not to worry. She tried to keep busy with our children and prayed lots. Some folk from the mission checked on them and assured them that delays could often happen up in the mountains.

The next day I spoke to my area manager and Abe. I told them clearly that I was a volunteer who had come to help and I was not prepared to contribute to the delinquency of others. I also told them that I would never go on another trip like that again. They realized that I was very unhappy.

I never went on an overnight trip again.

Funny, that seemed to be a big problem for me at the time and God was faithful and brought me home safely. God is still on His throne. He's big enough to take care of me now.

Chapter 16

APARTHEID

It did not matter to me if people thought I was foolish. I knew we must go back as planned. No matter what was happening in Maseru, I had to go back. I knew Charles was expecting me to come to him.

With the political unrest in LeSotho, outbursts of violence against foreigners or well-to-do locals were not uncommon. The LeSotho government constantly took the stance of an independent country that needed no help from the outside. This position caused problems that resulted in border closers and slowdowns and, often, violent attacks against any foreigners in the country.

I started asking myself, "Why did I come home without Charles? Stop it Betty. You know we talked about it and agreed we should go." Barry had bought a new home and asked if we could help him get settled in his new place. Tina wanted to come with and both Charles and Tina's husband thought it best if just 'we women' went to help Barry at this time. Charles felt he could not leave at this time and urged us to go. Now, I almost wished I had prayed about it more.

Two days before our scheduled departure date the American Embassy called and said we must leave Lesotho immediately, because they believed that fighting would start and the borders could be closed the next day. We packed and left. Now I really did not want to leave Charles. He insisted that we go and he assured me he would be fine and would leave at the first sign of trouble. I begged him to be very careful and not to take any chances. My mind was racing.

My thoughts slipped back to our first days in this new type of prejudice...

The M.C.C. volunteer group we were with was very unpopular with the South African government because of its stand against Apartheid. Apartheid was a system of laws similar to America's Jim Crow laws, although there was no attempt to hide the fact that the races were separated but not equal.

Lesotho was completely landlocked by South Africa and almost everything in Lesotho came from South Africa. So, when it came time to buy a new car for M.C.C., ironically enough, we were the only ones who could go to South Africa to do the job. The other volunteers could not obtain visas. Since we came to Lesotho with a three month visa for South Africa, we were chosen to go and buy the new car. At the time, we had no idea what that meant. We were about to find out.

When we arrived at the border, there was a long line (called a queue in Africa) waiting to cross. After about two hours of standing in that line, we finally received clearance to cross the border. We had not driven too long before we noticed the difference in the landscape of the two nations. In South Africa, there was more foliage. Everything was green and lush. The contrast between the poverty of Lesotho and prosperity of South Africa struck us immediately.

It took us only about fifteen minutes to arrive in Ladybrand, a town of about 3,500 people. And since the town was so small, we had no difficulty in finding the car dealership where we were to pick up the car.

The people at the dealership were expecting us. They served us tea and showed us the car. We would need to wait a little while as they finished the preparation and completed the paperwork.

While we sat and drank our tea, we noticed that people were coming up front to have a look at us. It was amusing, as people took too long to take a drink, or tie their shoe, or just boldly stare in our direction. We decided rather than sit and become a show piece on display, we would just take a walk uptown. As we headed up the street, we couldn't help but notice that we were, indeed, a curiosity. Just as we were about to cross one of the main streets, a car went past. The driver began to stare dumb-founded in our direction, as if he were seeing something impossible. Unfortunately, as he continued to stare, he forgot to watch where he was going and came within inches of hitting a lamp post. Barry and Tina couldn't control their laughter as the driver tried to correct his direction.

This entire experience was proving to be quite interesting to us, so we decided to go to the local butcher shop. Inside the shop, the customer area was divided in two by a rail. We had no idea what the rail was for, or which side of the rail we were expected to be on.

When an older lady walked into the shop, I whispered to her, "Ma'am, why is this rail here?

She looked at us, somewhat surprised. "Well, the 'blanks' (white people) are served on this side and the black Africans are served over there."

"Oh."

"You're not from around here, are you?"

"No, we're from America. We're serving in Maseru."

"Oh, that's very nice," she replied in a patronizing voice.

Later, we went to the post office. That was even worse. There were two separate unmarked doors. We just chose one door. Of course it was the wrong one. There were no white people on that side of the post office except for the employees. You could have heard a pin drop. We were met with nothing but incredulous stares. No one said a word. They just stared.

Slowly we walked out of the door and found the other side. We were served, but this time the stares were rude and condescending.

We noticed quickly that all service stations had two sets of washrooms. There were men's and women's washrooms with white signs and men's and women's washrooms with blue signs. Those with the white signs were for white people, and those with blue signs were for non-whites. When we had to use the washrooms, I took our children by the hand and took them into the wash room with the white signs. Again we received many contemptuous stares, but no one said a thing to us.

After this, our first real contact with South Africa, we took our car and went back to Lesotho.

We entered our director's office with the keys to the car. He looked up. "Oh, so you're back. How was it?"

By this time, several people from M.C.C. had gathered around us to hear the story.

"It was like a circus," Charles chuckled, "and we were the main act!"

This brought a roar of laughter from everyone there.

Our director's wife came in with a smile on her face. "We're just about ready for lunch. Come join us and tell us all about it."

Over a steaming bowl of Borsch and homemade bread, we began to recount our adventure.

There was a lot of laughter when we described our feelings as we went into the post office and when the man almost wrecked his car looking at us. Charles related that while we were waiting for our car he noticed that one of the workers came toward us and then stopped to tie his shoe. It was so obvious that he needed a better look at this strange family in the waiting room. We all kept laughing as Charles continued to share.

Everyone was pleased with the car that we brought back. We were just glad to be out of South Africa and back into Lesotho.

Chapter 17

LANGUAGE STUDY

Before we arrived in Lesotho we read that English was the second language. Therefore, we assumed that most people in Lesotho were bi-lingual. In schools, the lower grades were taught in Sesotho while the upper grades were taught in English. Most of those who completed the upper grades had some understanding of the English language, but few were fluent. Sometimes, we became frustrated when we could not communicate.

Our mission arranged for us to spend a few weeks with Ntate and Me' Mahono in the village of Tabola to study Sesotho. It took us about an hour and a half to drive to Tabola. Tabola was barely a village. It had no stores, no post office, just a little gathering of houses. It made me wonder how it even got a name. Nearby, Peka, a more identifiable village, had a post office and even a café with canned goods, fresh foods, and refrigeration!

To get to Tabola, we drove through a rather desolate landscape. There were many dongas – deep gullies some-times forty feet deep–formed by erosion. One of the early assignments of the Soil Conservation project was to try to re-forest these areas with trees. At first, the seeds were eaten by animals, but eventually the department of Agriculture raised nurseries of trees for transplanting. Then, the areas were fenced to protect the trees–mimosa, cottonwood and poplar–until they were big enough to survive. In five years, these reclaimed dongas became little forests.

Ntate Mahono was a pastor of one of the Independent churches in Lesotho. We stayed in their rondoval, a beautiful round stone building with a thatch roof. It had no electricity, telephone, or water. We carried water in a bucket from the pump not far from our house. We cooked on a small gas camp stove. We ate a lot of beans and greens during those next few weeks. Sometimes we bought bread from the café in Peka. We used to stop on Sundays and get hot bread fresh out of the oven. We'd take it home and eat it right away with cheese.

Every morning we had lessons with Ntate or Me' Mahono. In the afternoons we studied to prepare for our Sesotho language meetings together in the evenings. While we worked to learn, Barry and Tina, who were about five and six, played outside with the sheep, goats, chickens, horses, dogs, donkeys and cows. They had a wonderful new adventure every day. They came in at night covered in dirt. All you could see were their eyeballs and their smiles. The custom there was to sweep up the outdoor yard every day, which put a lot more dirt into the already dusty air. The worst part was that we had no way to bathe them! We simply used a wash pan.

Most of the village children never wore any clothes at all until about the age of five. Sometimes they would wear a short little t-shirt. Babies did not even wear nappies. When it was chilly in the mornings, the children wrapped themselves in a blanket. Many people wore blankets all the time, even in 80 degree weather. And, as cold as it could sometimes be, no one wore shoes. Their feet became hardened.

The people capitalized on the sunshine, washing children on the east side of the their homes in the morning and sitting on the west side of their homes in the evenings. At night, when the temperature sometimes dropped down to 25 degrees, the people lit fires in buckets inside their rondovals. It would appear as if their homes were on fire as the smoke seeped out around the roof and rafters. Inside, the smoke hung thick around the ceiling.

Our lessons continued on a daily basis. Lesotho, pronounced l'soo-too, is the country. Basotho is a group of people from Lesotho. A Mosotho is a single individual from Lesotho, and the language spoken is Sesotho.

Between lessons, we spent most of the time engaged in survival tasks. By the time I washed the dishes, the clothes, and the children, there was little time left for study. While doing our laundry in a tub out in the warm sunshine, a big lazy-looking cow meandered over to take a drink from my washtub. I was busy hanging clothing on the line when Barry and Tina yelled, "Look Mom! The cow is eating our clothes!"

I looked over just in time to see that cow chewing on one of our tea towels. The children thought this was very funny. I grabbed the piece of towel hanging from the cow's mouth and pulled as hard as I could. The cow threw its head back and walked away, still chewing my towel. I watched in complete disbelief as the cow continued to consume our dish towel. I wondered if this would make the cow sick. Ntate Mahono assured us no damage was done, except we were missing a towel.

In spite of all of the menial chores, we had a delightful time walking through the village trying to speak to everyone we met. I'm sure we were comical to the villagers trying to communicate in their language. Most of the time they were very polite, but occasionally they couldn't suppress a giggle when we said something wrong.

At night, the sky became our entertainment. There were no streetlights to dim the brilliance of the stars or interfere with our view. We had never seen such a big sky, so full of massive stars that looked like spotlights. They seemed so close you felt you grab a handful and put them in your pocket. We delighted in the display of northern lights and Haley's comet. Most people will never see anything like this.

One of the first customs that Ntate Mahono taught us was that it was very important among the Basotho people to properly greet each other before–long before–stating any business or a reason for visiting. And when visiting someone, you must never state that you are leaving. You must always ask permission to leave. These were two important rules of etiquette amongst these people.

Women always carried their babies on their backs and loads on their heads. They eagerly taught me to carry a bucket of water on my head. Unlike the language, I learned this skill pretty quickly. We learned that married women never showed their knees. Women in the villages always wore dresses or skirts, never pants. A woman would never go to church with bare arms, or a sleeveless dress. However, they would nurse their babies openly at any time or any place and think nothing of it.

When I asked about this I was told that the breast is the tool God gave to women to provide for their children. Eventually we grew accustomed to this and learned not to judge them by our standards.

Me' Mahono shared with us this story that happened to her the week before we came to them.

She and Ntate had gone to get some supplies. While Ntate was in the bank she shopped at the market. A young man wielding a knife cornered her and demanded all her money. She quickly handed him her bag. He took all the money and returned the purse and said, "Now, Mommy, give me what's in the dairy!" She reached into her bosom and gave him the rest of her money. He ran and left her unharmed. She went on to explain to us that it is safer to carry significant monies in the bosom, rather than the purse, because of pick pockets.

Another custom we learned was that if there were only a few chairs in the room, the men always sat in the chairs while the women and children sat on the floor. The men would be fed first after which the women and children were allowed to eat. If a guest or a white man would visit, he, of course would be fed first. He and his family would be seated at the table. The Basotho would not usually eat with them, but would eagerly serve them. This was considered a sign of respect.

If a guest, a foreigner, or a white man would visit a church, he would be taken to the front of the church and be expected to sit on the platform behind the preacher. They were expected to exhort and encourage the congregation, and would always be asked to speak.

That first Sunday, we went to church with them Me' Mahono introduced us to the congregation. She said, "These are our very dear friends from America. They are man and wife. Remember, when God created Eve, He took a rib from Adam's side and He formed Eve. Me' Betty is the rib of Ntate Charles and she is his helpmeet. Let's welcome them to our church this morning." The reason she explained this was to prepare the people for us—a mixed race couple—something the people had never seen before.

With that, the congregation stood and sang a song in Sesotho in our honor.

When Charles spoke to the congregation, he used an interpreter. He greeted everyone in the name of Jesus Christ, our Lord and Savior. He then thanked everyone for all of their help in teaching us some of their customs and encouraging us to speak Sesotho. He shared with them the love of Jesus Christ based on John 3:16. At the end when he asked if anyone wanted to receive Jesus as their Lord and Savior, everyone responded. After everyone prayed together, I led them in a Sesotho chorus of rejoicing. It was well over an hour before we were finished. After the service, everyone thanked us for the excellent service, but mentioned that it had been far too short. We wondered about this. Later on we found that most African services start at about 11:00 in the morning and go on until 4:00 or 5:00 that afternoon. Almost everyone in the service gets up to share together the goodness of God in their lives and praises Him for some way that He has blessed them in the past week.

What wonderful friends the Mahono's became to us. Occasionally Me' Mahono would come to help us with our play day. No one could tell a Bible story in Sesotho like Me' Mahono. The children listened enraptured by her expression and animation. She truly had a deep love for the Word of God.

Throughout our five-week stay we learned more and more of the Sesotho language, but among us, only Tina became truly fluent. Charles and I learned to use an interpreter when we preached.

What wonderful experiences Charles and I had together with the people of Lesotho. How could this beautiful people be under such attack? I knew without a doubt that God wanted me back in Africa. Our task was not completed. And now, more than ever, there remained work to do.

Chapter 18

BATTLE ZONE

As the explosions, both small arms fire and artillery fire, continued to rattle the house, I wondered what the American Embassy was doing. Were they actively putting together a plan? I would wait to hear from them a little longer.

We had never called on them for help before, although there had been other times when it might have been advisable. We simply didn't have a phone back then. I remembered the danger that we had all faced together early on.

It was March of 1980. The Apartheid struggles in South Africa were beginning to escalate. The ANC (African National Congress) was the most militant force trying to overthrow the existing government. As their efforts inten-sified, the South African Government became more and more vicious in trying to quell the rebellion and to main-tain the status quo. So, frequently, rebels from South Africa who were wanted by their government would seek asylum in neighboring countries, such as Lesotho, Botswana, and Trans Kei. There was much sympathy for their cause in Lesotho, so they didn't have much trouble finding asylum.

South Africa responded by cracking down at border crossings. Border guards carefully scrutinized every person. You had to present your passport, which they would carry back to another room to compare it against a list of names. The added security increased the time spent on each individual, resulting in huge lines of people waiting for permission to come into or out of South Africa. It was especially difficult to cross with a vehicle. Sometimes the guards would unload every bag or box on a truck, setting the contents out in the sun. If the goods were milk or perishables, they would be ruined. At these times, only two or three trucks or cars actually made it in or out of Lesotho.

Although South Africa could not legally close the border, they made commerce very difficult between the two countries. Lesotho, landlocked by South Africa, was totally dependent on incoming goods, Many people commuted daily from Lesotho to South Africa to work. The South African border crackdown was their way of putting pressure on the country of Lesotho.

Each time we crossed, we would park the car and get in line to have our passport stamped. We quickly learned that the old adage, "You can catch more flies with honey than with vinegar" definitely applied at the border crossings. Unbeknownst to Betty, I gave in to convenience and occasionally paid off the guards on the Lesotho side to ease the process of bringing in goods – even groceries. If you had a good reputation with the guards, you got in and out much easier – with no inspections. Officially, no one was allowed to bring in from South Africa anything that was produced in Lesotho, such as eggs or bread. We became good friends with the border guards for both Lesotho and South Africa.

Once, we made a trip to Swaziland. The Swaziland border crossing authorities told us we must leave our straw hats and drinks at the border. So we stood beside the car, drank our cool drinks and left our hats. Another time at the Botswana border, we were required to drive through a solution of some sort. Then they asked us to get out and walk through the same solution. We later learned that an epidemic of hoof and mouth disease in the livestock had broken out there.

In addition to the unrest in South Africa, turmoil increased in Lesotho itself. Governed by an elected parliament, as well as a king and queen, elections were called in the country whenever the ruling government saw fit to do so. An 'Opposition' party existed who sought to overthrow the standing government by violent means. They wanted definite election dates as well as power. People who adhered to this party wore red and black blankets as a symbol of their stand against the government.

One day we were shopping when we came across a red blanket that caught Betty's eye. We decided to buy it. When we went to pay for it, a lady approached us and said, "You may want to choose another blanket. That one represents opposition to the government." We decided not to buy the blanket.

Sometimes riots spontaneously erupted in the streets when people from the opposition party attempted to storm the palace. They would push into the gates of the palace, usually blocking streets and traffic for blocks. If a car happened to be in the area at the time, they would often throw bricks and stones at it and turn it on its side. Many frightened people ran from the area in mass hysteria toward the mountains shouting, "Run. They're shooting everyone."

Most of the time, the soldiers simply shot into the air. But, if the rebellion continued, they would turn their weapons onto the crowds. In their panic, people were frequently injured while trying to flee from the violence in town.

We always tried to avoid being caught in the madness, even though no one seemed to know how or when it would happen.

The school our kids attended was located right behind the palace. When the violence erupted, the school administrators would dismiss the students to go home, releasing them into all the craziness. Fortunately, missionary friends of ours always took our kids in until we could get to them.

One particular night that March, we were sleeping soundly when a terrific explosion occurred close by. It felt like it was right outside our door.

We heard the whirling and clatter of helicopter blades almost directly above our house. Terrified, Barry and Tina ran into our room crying, "Daddy, Mommy, are we going to die?" We held them close to us and began to pray.

Slowly and cautiously, I crept to the window to see what was happening. Huddled behind me, Betty also looked out. A huge army helicopter flew overhead very low with a large spotlight shining on the houses in our neighborhood. Another loud explosion shook our house so badly that we were sure that the windows would break. Immediately afterward we heard the sound of automatic gunfire all around our house.

We bolted away from the window and pressed our bodies flat on the floor along with Barry and Tina. We lay motionless there for what seemed to be hours.

Eventually it grew quiet. We did not move, but continued to lie on the floor praying with our arms around the children.

At about three o'clock we climbed back into bed. Barry and Tina did not want to leave us, so they slept with us that night. These scriptures rose up in my spirit: Psalms 121:5-6 "The Lord is thy keeper: the Lord is thy shade upon thy right hand. The sun shall not smite thee by day, nor the moon by night." We fell into a fitful sleep.

When we awoke the next morning, the sun shone brightly. As usual, we prepared to take Barry and Tina to school. As we were leaving we saw the neighbor next door.

"Hey, what happened last night?"

She shrugged her shoulders.

"I mean the explosions. Didn't you hear all of the explosions?"

"I didn't hear anything."

The look on her face told us that she really did not want to talk about it.

I looked at Betty, "Maybe Me' Mathabo will talk about it."

We knocked at her door. She looked out.

"Me' Mathabo, did you hear all of those explosions last night?"

She gave us that blank look. "I hear nothing last night."

At that point we had no more time to talk to neighbors who heard nothing. We had to be on our way. We jumped into the car and rushed into Maseru. Just past the gate of our compound we were horrified to see that an entire house had been blown away. It was only about five houses from ours.

When we arrived at the office, the M.C.C. staff was watching the South African news on the television. Apparently, the South African government had crossed into Lesotho and other neighboring countries to capture or kill South African refugees from the ANC. At least in our neighborhood they had been quite successful. Several people had been killed in the attack. Also, the main post office in Maseru had been destroyed.

No one in the area would acknowledge the attack or talk about politics in general for fear that they would be talking to an informant. A few days later, we saw pictures of a crib still standing in the destroyed house. The baby had been shot. Blood was spattered everywhere.

This began a decade of escalating hostilities between the two factions in South Africa. Lesotho also saw its share of hostilities from the opposition party. It became a way of life for us. Yet we feared no evil because God was with us. He had led us here, and we were determined to fight the fight of faith while the world battled each other around us. But we had not seen the last of it.

Chapter 19

HOME AND BACK

In June of 1981, we flew back to the United States and Canada for our first home leave. We planned it that way to avoid the Lesotho winter, and to be in the United States and Canada during the summer. During that time we were to reconnect with friends and family. We hoped to speak about our work wherever we could.

We had prepared a slide show to present to different churches where we had been asked to speak. Because we sat through so many of these presentations in the past and hadn't been very impressed, we were determined to make ours as interesting and fun as we could.

It took us about a week to put the show together. Instead of having a script that we would read from, we made a tape using all of our voices. This also kept the slide show from rambling or dragging.

We tried to keep it as enjoyable as we could. For example, after a slide from play day, we would suddenly have a full face slide of Charles pulling one of Barry's baby teeth, with Barry's little high voice saying, "It's hard to find a dentist in Lesotho!"

Our first stop was Chester to visit with our families. I took Betty and our children with me, no more me going to my home and Betty's brother meeting her and taking her to her home. I had a new sister-in-law. When we met the first time, she thought there should be a write-up about us and our work in the local paper. The following day, a reporter came to Mom's house, took pictures of us and wrote a very nice article. That seemed to close all the doors of prejudice in our home town forever.

We had a great time talking, visiting, playing and enjoying ourselves with all of them. They had so many questions about our lifestyle there–how and where we lived, and what we did from one day to the next. Many of our nieces and nephews were very curious about what kinds of animals we saw, and if we were in danger of being eaten by lions. They all laughed about my first trip into the mountains. We talked about play day, and many of our friends. However, we could tell that all of our families were a little uncomfortable with our being there, so we avoided the stories of the bombings by South Africa and the times when we were in danger.

We never stopped to rest on that trip. There were too many people to see, too much to do, too many churches to visit. We ate too much and slept too little. We realized while we in the U.S., that we were extremely happy in Africa, and the work we were involved in there.

After about six or seven weeks of traveling and visiting between Chester and St. Louis, we took a trip to visit old friends and acquaintances in Kitchener. Our slide show received rave reviews. It was wonderful to get back together with friends who had accepted us for who we were back in the days when our marriage was so difficult in the United States.

At the end of our leave, we went to Chicago to catch our flight home. As usual, it was a long flight back. After the whirlwind we had just been through, it was a relief to take advantage of this time to pray and spend time reading our Bibles. As the rest of the family slept, I reflected on the wonderful blessings that God had given us. Not only had He taught us new things in this new land, but he also used us in so many different ways. I eagerly looked forward to returning to Lesotho. After two months away from my work and our home, I wondered in what condition we'd find them.

By the time we reached Johannesburg, we were all exhausted from the eighteen hour flight. We expected to have about a four hour layover and then we would continue to fly to Maseru.

The plane going from Jo'burg to Maseru was a small turboprop with about twelve other passengers. We boarded at about eleven o'clock in the morning. Betty and I sat in the front seats while Barry and Tina sat together a few rows back. Exhausted, I closed my eyes before the engines started. Just as the pilot started the engines, Barry cried "FIRE!" Everyone on the plane looked out to see the right wing in flames as the pilot jumped out of the cockpit to fight the fire.

Our hearts sank as we watched him extinguish the fire. Feeling exhausted and helpless, we wondered what we were going to do. The pilot instructed us all to go back to the airport and wait. When we arrived, we heard the announcement that there would be another flight to Maseru at four o'clock in the afternoon. Barry and Tina fell asleep as Betty and I became more fatigued with each passing moment. We had been without sleep for more than 28 hours.

Four o'clock came and went and nothing happened. At that point, we discovered that the plane that had caught fire was the same plane scheduled to make the afternoon flight to Lesotho. We decided we must try to find something to eat. After a light snack, we started feeling better, but still wondered, along with everyone else, how we would ever get to Lesotho. The airline announced that there would be a flight provided – but no one seemed to know how or when.

As the afternoon turned into evening a man from the airlines came through and announced that they had chartered a special plane and that we should prepare to board. It was now nine at night. What they chartered was an old DC3. It even had drapes on the windows.

Our plane flew so low that we could see the lights from every little town that we flew over. It was a noisy flight, but fascinating. We were just happy to finally be going home. It took about forty-five minutes longer than usual to get to Maseru.

When the pilot announced that we would be landing in about ten minutes, we began to look for the airport. I was next to the window. I could not see any landing lights. This began to concern me.

The plane continued to descend, but all we saw below was darkness. Finally I said to Betty softly, "Something is wrong. I can't see anything down there, no landing lights, not even any lights in the airport building. Everything is black."

As I continued to look, suddenly I saw a green light and I exclaimed to Betty, "Wait a minute, now I can see some little green runway lights."

As soon as I said that, the plane touched down. As the plane taxied to the terminal we peered out of the windows, looking for some sign of lights or life, but still could see nothing but blackness. Finally the plane came to a stop somewhere in the middle of the darkness. Within a few minutes, two local men boarded the plane with flashlights and said, "Each and every passenger must give us your passport before leaving the plane. We have no electricity and cannot process your passports tonight. You may come back tomorrow to collect your luggage and your passports."

Most of the people on the plane began to murmur and complain, but we were just too tired. We turned in our passports and disembarked. As we put our feet on the tarmac, we heard a familiar high-pitched voice shouting, "Welcome back, McGee's. We're glad you're back."

When we looked in that direction all we could see was flashlights. Soon we were greeted by hugs and kisses from many of our friends. We didn't know who was hugging and kissing who since it was so dark. As we trekked through the airport, we found ourselves stepping over broken bricks, glass, concrete, metal frames, and other assorted debris. We held each others hands tightly and we each held our children's hands.

Our friends drove us to their home. After eating a nice hot meal and enjoying a fresh cup of tea we learned that the airport had been blown away. Apparently a homemade bomb had been left inside the airport and blew the building to pieces. Officials weren't sure who had done it, but they suspected that it was the opposition party because they had been demanding that the Government hold elections. So far these demands had not even been considered.

We had been at the airport in Johannesburg almost all day and we had not been very happy about it or very patient after having traveled so far. Yet God knew. Did He delay our plane? Did He once again make a way to keep us from all harm?

Lord, forgive us for murmuring and help us to praise You always for Your perfect timing wherever we go.

It was good to be home and in our own bed. With prayers of thanks on my lips, I slipped into a deep and peaceful sleep.

God had moved in a supernatural way to protect us back then. Surely, He will protect me now.

Chapter 20

SURPRISES

Now that I was determined to return to South Africa I felt better. I just wished Charles would call and tell me he was safely out of Maseru. I whispered a quick prayer, "Lord, please get him out of there and have him call me before we leave."

I was trying desperately to keep fear away from me. It can attack with such force. But, I was no stranger to this battle. I had defeated it before.

Three weeks after we had arrived in Maseru, I had to collect the children from school. At the time I was driving the Nomad. I had letters piled on the front seat that I promised to mail at the post office. Of course they were lying there unsecured and uncontained. I was only a block away from the M.C.C. office turning onto a side street. When I turned, those letters slid to the floor. I lunged to grab them, but I missed. Suddenly, my left front wheel fell into the ditch by the side of the road. Panicking, I jerked the steering wheel hard to the right. Hitting a large culvert, the Nomad flipped onto its right side and slid to a stop. I had no seat belt on. I found myself with my feet against the door on the ground and my back against the front seat. My knee was bleeding badly.

I stayed motionless in that position, trying to think of what to do. Still a little dazed, I looked out the windshield to see many, dark faces speaking to me in a language that I could not understand. The scene became one huge, confusing kaleidoscope as everything around me turned into a blur of color and voices.

As I struggled to regain my bearings, I felt the car move. My heart jumped as I thought that the car may be turning completely over on its roof. All I heard was "Okay mommy, okay mommy." The people together turned the car upright, where it landed on all four wheels with a thud. Still shocked from the whole ordeal, I sat up in the seat. From there, they helped me from the car, all the while excitedly shouting in broken English, "Car okay! You okay!" The car was not okay. It was not even drivable.

My knee had a pretty bad gash in it which continued to bleed. Our friends in the mission office had heard the commotion, recognized the car, and came running. Putting me in one of their cars, they wanted to take me to the hospital. But I was still concerned about getting Barry and Tina. One of them, I don't remember who, assured me that they would take care of that for me

I still refused to go to the hospital. The main reason was that we had frequently gone to Maseru hospital to minister to patients there. The conditions were deplorable. After those visits, and our ordeal with Tina, I vowed that I would never go to one of those places. I had no confidence that one could ever get better, or even live through an experience in one of these hospitals.

One Sunday, shortly after we returned from our first home leave, we invited several people to our home for lunch. While I prepared the meal, I began to feel uncomfortable. I became just a little nauseated and slightly dizzy. After everything was ready, we sat down to eat holding hands for the prayer and then passing the food around.

The first bite I took hit my stomach like a rock. I couldn't eat any more. The rest of the meal I just pushed the food around on my plate and kept conversing with my friends. As I cleared the table and began to do the dishes, I noticed a sharp pain developing in my lower right abdomen that progressively grew worse.

As soon as we bade the last person good-bye and shut the door, I looked at Charles and said, "Honey, I don't feel very well."

"You didn't seem to be yourself at dinner. What's the matter?"

"It's my lower right side, right here," I said, pointing to where the pain was coming from.

"I think we better go see the doctor."

I didn't argue. The pain intensified.

As we drove down the bumpy road, my body felt more tender with every bump. When we found the doctor, he examined me and then asked me to jump up and down. With the first jump I crumpled to the floor in pain.

He said, "Go home and lie down for two or three hours. If it is not better, then you come back."

I went home and things just deteriorated from bad to worse. Finally Charles said, "I'm not waiting any longer. We need to go now."

When we showed up again at the doctor's house, he met us at the door. "Don't wait any longer. You need to go to the hospital. You have appendicitis."

Even through my pain, I groaned. "I'm not going to that hospital!"

"There is a mission hospital in Morija. It's better. Go there."

We headed for Morija, a forty-five minute drive, again driving over that bumpy road. I was in agony. By the time we got to the tarmac the sun was beginning to set. Visibility was poor, so Charles had to drive slowly. We had not driven too far when we noticed something looming in the road ahead. Fortunately, Charles stopped the car before hitting it. When we were close enough, we could see that it was a car that had literally run over a herd of sheep. Several sheep lie dead under the car and it was unable to move. We slowly eased past this accident and continued on to the hospital in Morija.

We arrived and hesitantly entered the emergency room. The doctor in charge grabbed a bloody sheet off the examining table saying, "Excuse the mess. We just treated a stab wound."

He proceeded to examine me and found it to be my appendix. He would have to operate immediately. Charles and I stopped to pray. I did not like the looks of anything around me. I did not want to be here.

Nurses put me onto a metal gurney and rolled me outside and into the surgery building where they administered the anesthesia and proceeded to remove my appendix. They told Charles that it should all be over in about an hour, and to just relax. Three and a half hours later, the doctor came out to Charles and said that they had found that the appendix was attached to the lower bowel, which made its removal much more difficult. He had had to call another doctor in to assist him because he was having some trouble with it.

He also told Charles that because I was no longer young, I would have to stay in the hospital for about ten days. He wanted me to rest. Although the appendix had not burst, the doctor wanted to keep an eye on me.

After the surgery, the doctor assigned me to a private room all by myself. I saw no one. No food came. I didn't even see a nurse for at least three or four days. The only people I saw were Charles and the kids. Each time they came I praised God for them. They brought food to me.

I had been put on an IV drip, but something went wrong and my arm began to swell. I tried to get up, but could not. I screamed several times to see if anyone could hear me and would come in.

Finally a nurse came in and saw me trying to get up. "You may not get up!"

"But look at my arm. It's swelling. Can't you do something?"

"I'll be back."

I waited for over five hours. Finally, Charles came. He took one look at my arm and went to get the doctor. The doctor removed the IV immediately. Unfortunately, a permanent lump resulted from the swelling.

I felt very alone and isolated in the hospital. All I wanted to do was go home, but I had to lie flat on my back for ten days. It seemed like ten years. Finally I was able to go home, but the doctor made me promise to stay in bed for two more weeks. At least I could get up and walk to the bathroom, but not for more than ten or fifteen minutes at a time.

Like Job, the thing I feared is what came upon me. I had to be in a local hospital.

During my recovery, our friends faithfully came to see me. Jill was a daily visitor. Ntate and Me' Mahono stopped by. During the two play days when I was confined to bed, I had to watch out the window while my friends took charge. I really wanted to be outside with them.

One evening, John and Patty came by. They brought their usual sack of joy with them.

"How's the sick girl?" John teased me.

"I'm not too happy about having to stay in bed."

"Ah, I brought you something to cheer you up."

"Oh?"

"I know how much you miss playing the piano."

He was definitely right about that. If there was one thing I truly missed from the civilized world, it was my piano.

"Well, we couldn't get a piano in our little car, so I thought you might like this." He pulled a guitar into the bedroom door.

"Well, I don't know how to play..."

"Then you'll have to learn."

"Hmmm," I mused. "How hard is it?"

"It's a breeze. Here. I'll show you how to play a song with just three chords. Do you know "Praise The Name Of Jesus?"

That was one of my favorite songs.

When they left, I started to practice what John had shown me on the guitar. I practiced "Praise the Name of Jesus" until my fingers ached. By the third week it was beginning to sound like a real song. Within another week I was using the guitar to sing songs with our play day group. It's amazing how many songs have just three chords. After awhile I learned more chords and was able to lead singing for praise and worship at our services.

Now I praised God for His goodness to me. Not only was I singing and playing a new instrument, but I was healed and whole and feeling well again.

Chapter 21

CHANGES

Over the next couple of years we found the Lord calling us to expand our ministries in Lithabaneng. We ministered to about 300 children per week through our play day. One of the women who helped in our play day was Jill, a nurse from Canada who had a heart of gold and a true spirit for service.

After each play day we had a substantial amount of cleanup to do. We had to put the arts and crafts away. And, there was always some food mess to clean up, which is to be expected after 300 children have been active in one area for several hours.

One day, Jill and I cleaned up together, putting art supplies back into the storage shed. I always enjoyed her company because she was just so easy to get along with. At some point in our conversation she stated, "You know, Betty, I'd really, like to work some with the leper mission up the road."

I knew exactly what she was talking about. On the road leading from the east of Maseru into the countryside was a large mountain on the left and Lithabaneng on the right. At the base of this mountain was the leper mission. Farther up the road, around the mountain was an army post.

I suggested, "Why don't we go there and try to make some arrangements with them?"

The following week, we went to the mission and asked the management if we could be of some help. They were thrilled to accept our offer.

Every Monday morning we would go to the leper mission in the morning. We served tea and cookies, knit and crocheted with some of the patients, and taught a Bible study. We continued this ministry for as long as we were in Lithabaneng. We always spoke Sesotho with those people. Both Jill and I became better in the language as a result.

Strange things often happened in our neighborhood in Lithabaneng. One evening while we were in our house, we heard a car outside, and then a slight knock at the door. When we answered, a man who did not speak English motioned for us to come outside. He led us to his car, still running and with the lights on. Immediately in front of the car was the body of a woman sprawled on the ground, face down.

Our first thought was that he had struck her with his car in the dark. Quickly seeking to bridge the communication gap, we found a neighbor who understood English and acted as our interpreter. We found that the woman had not been struck by the car after all. An alcoholic, she had been walking home when she tripped and struck her head on a rock. There was a pretty nasty gash on her forehead.

"If you know her, could you take her home?" Charles asked.

"Oh, no. She is the wife of Abraham. Abraham is a very jealous man. If I bring her home he may beat me."

Charles said, "Well he won't beat me. I'll take her home."

Charles was confident, not just because he was bigger than most of the Basotho people, but he was also known throughout the area as a man of God. So together, he and I returned the woman to her home. He seemed very grateful that we would be kind enough to bring her home. We prayed with them. I don't know what happened after that, because we never saw them again.

On another occasion during our play day, a lady collapsed on the dirt road in front of our house. Her lady companion ran to us for help. Quickly, Charles picked her up and put her in our car, a Volkswagen Beetle. We had to take Barry and Tina with us, so we had six in the car, counting the children. They scrunched up behind the back seat in the little cubbyhole that they called the "doggie house." Off we went to the hospital, praying all the way. I checked her for vital signs and found none. She began to lose body fluids in our car. Her companion began to wail, knowing that she was dead. When we arrived, we went straight to the emergency room and carried her in. Her friend was so distraught that we stayed, attempting to console her. Eventually, the lady who had collapsed regained consciousness. It turned out that she had extremely high blood pressure. The attending physician said that she was lucky to be alive. We knew that luck had nothing to do with it. All of us prayed together, praising God for His goodness, and we took the other lady home.

One evening it started raining just before dark. The rain on the tin roof was loud, but steady and soothing. We decided to turn in early. At about one in the morning Charles and I both awoke, rather suddenly. It was still raining. We wondered what woke us. We began to talk softly in our bedroom. All of a sudden we heard our dog barking furiously. We jumped out of bed and headed into the living room. We were stunned at what we saw.

There were candles on the floor. They had been used for light. Food had been left on the floor and the fridge door was open. The kid's books were scattered all over the floor. Most disturbing of all were the big muddy footprints on the window sill, on the sofa and on the floor. The footprints went right up to our bedroom door and in front of the children's bedroom door. The back door stood open. And, our dog was still barking furiously.

We had been robbed! We could hardly believe it. The kid's backpacks were gone. My carry-all bag was gone. Food was gone. However, since we always kept our purses and wallets in our bedroom, they were safe.

At daybreak we contacted the local police and most all of our neighbors came to say how sorry they were and to see how much damage had been done. Charles and the police followed the muddy footprints to a house not far from us. No one was home. We looked in the window and saw some of our things in that house. The police said they would check later in the day in hopes that someone would be home. We went back to that same house in the afternoon and it had been cleared out. No one was there and nothing was left inside

We were just grateful to God that those muddy footprints had stopped outside of our bedroom door and that no one was hurt.

At the end of four years, the second part of Charles' two-year contracts with the Lesotho government ended. He experienced continual frustration in his job. Every time he found a way to improve the situation, he was blocked by government bureaucracy. They weren't interested in innovation, just in maintaining the status quo. Our friend, Bill, suggested that Charles work at another garage and Charles was interested. Bill came to visit us one Friday afternoon and said, "There's the M.E.L. Garage in Morija. It was set up by some Dutch people and funded for three years for the L.E.C. (Lesotho Evangelical Church) just to maintain their own cars. I think S.E.V.A. (Swiss Evangelical Mission) had some input into it as well. The three years aree almost up now and the church would love to keep it going, but there is no funding. We were hoping that we could run it as a self-supporting operation, with no additional funding from anywhere."

Charles thought and prayed about this for some time. One of his biggest concerns was that M.E.L. would have to be efficient enough to support the operation and the employee's. Bill believed the garage was worth saving. He had been taking his own car there and it had always been well-serviced and well taken care of. Bill also knew Charles well and believed that he had the ability to manage this business successfully. Charles agreed to pursue the opportunity.

We sought the approval from M.C.C. for relocation. They expressed concern over the extra drive time and the increased wear and tear on the vehicles since I would have to maintain my employment in the M.C.C. office in Maseru. However, the drive was only about forty kilometers and the road between the two cities was not bad by Lesotho standards.

There was also a house for us in Morija. In fact, it was quite a step up from where we had lived in Lithabaneng. The place actually had a fenced-in yard with grass and plants. The garden was fabulous.

We decided to make the move. Morija was very different from Maseru and Lithabaneng. It contained only a couple of stores, a post office, the garage, a printing works, a hospital, several schools and a few missionary homes. We arrived during a water shortage so we had water from 6:00 to 7:00 in the morning and 6:00 to 7:00 at night, and no water on the weekends.

Our biggest problem developed over the lack of a decent education for Barry and Tina. While we were in Lithabaneng, they had attended classes at Maseru Prep, a school that maintained British educational standards. The school was excellent and kept the children challenged with the most modern learning. Barry and Tina had both flourished in this environment.

The school in Morija was the Morija English Medium School. Most of the people with whom we had spoken endorsed it as a good school. Unfortunately, we did not find this to be the case. We learned from Barry and Tina that this school wasn't what we had hoped for. Barry was quick with the answers in class, which did not make him too popular with the other students or even the teacher. At the same time, my daily drive to Maseru was taking its toll on me. To solve those problems, we decided to do home schooling. The solution worked out perfectly because M.C.C. had just changed administrators and my services at the office were no longer required.

Home schooling truly became a blessing. It gave us all a chance to bond in a different way. However, I quickly noticed that something was not quite right with Tina. She seemed to have some difficulty reading and wanted to write her numbers backward. After a short time, I called Charles' brother, Don, a teacher and coach in the States. Don spoke about our situation to his brother, Bill, who was also a teacher. Bill suggested that we set up an appointment for Tina to be evaluated in Springfield, Illinois by a specialist in that area on our next home leave. I continued to teach Tina until that time.

Charles eagerly set up shop in his new garage. He began to seek an efficient way to organize and inventory the parts department. Because we were so far from a parts supply, it became very important to stock the most popular parts.

His main challenge was to hire and train men to be mechanics to work at the garage. He decided to sponsor one student per year in trade school. On holidays and school vacations, they were employed by the garage. It wasn't long until he had several skilled, trained, mechanics.

We knew that our support from M.C.C. would only last another year. M.C.C. volunteers only served two three-year terms and we were in our fifth year. We also knew our support didn't really come from M.C.C.. Our help came from the Lord. He was just using M.C.C. as an instrument. As long as He wanted us here, He would provide a way for us.

Chapter 22

HEALED

Political unrest in Lesotho continued to increase. In April 1983, Lesotho's prime minister, Chief Leabua Jonathan, apparently made a statement to the National Assembly that Lesotho faced a war with South Africa. Shortly after that there were bomb explosions in Pretoria and Bloemfontein. We had heard that the ANC office in Lesotho claimed responsibility for the bombings and later denied any responsibility. We were unaware of the magnitude of problems this activity would cause at the border, but we were to find out quickly.

That May, I contracted Typhoid fever. After seeing Barry and Tina off to school in Morija, I went to Scott Hospital for tests and an examination.

While examining me, the doctor found a lump in my right breast as well as several under my right arm. He very kindly explained to me that I must go to Bloemfontein right away to be seen by a cancer specialist. The doctor explained his concern and the need for immediate treatment. If the lumps proved to be cancer, early treatment could save my life. As I sat in the chair listening to his words, his voice seemed to be far away. Fear began to engulf me. It started at my toes and moved up swiftly, causing a sharp pain in my stomach and choking the breath from me. I couldn't even swallow! In the distance I heard the doctor say, "I'll make all of the necessary arrangements for you, including your passage into South Africa because this is a medical emergency." At that time, we did not have visas for South Africa.

"Thank you," I weakly replied.

With that, I walked out of his office and went straight home. There I found Charles, Barry and Tina at home for lunch. As Charles looked up, he read my face perfectly. I fell into his arms weeping as I told him of how the doctor suspected cancer in my breast. We talked about it, ate lunch, and prayed together. After lunch, Charles went back to the garage while Barry and Tina returned to school.

I sat alone on an easy chair in the living room, trying to relax. I could not! Within a minute I was back up pacing the floor. I began to feel nauseated. Not knowing whether it was the Typhoid that was still with me or just the emotional stress, I felt my stomach bunch up.

I prayed, "Lord, why me? I had a biopsy just last October and it was fine. Why is it not fine now? Why has it grown? Am I going to lose this breast? Do I really have cancer? Why, Lord? Why?"

As I tried to pray I found that I could not concentrate. I opened the Word of God to Job only to find myself feeling worse, and even more frightened. I gave up. I had no peace. My mind was racing.

Again I spoke, "Lord, I am supposed to be a Christian. Who would know by looking at me now? How am I different from those who do not know you or who do not accept you? How am I different now? The way I feel now cannot be Your will for me. Again I opened the Word to Romans 12:12 and read: "Be joyful in hope, patient in affliction, faithful in prayer."

"Lord," I prayed, "I want to be, but I cannot! Surely this is not the way for a Christian to act. How did Paul do it?"

Again I opened my Bible to Ephesians 5 and read, "...
be filled with the spirit... Sing and make music in your heart
to the Lord, always giving thanks to God the Father for
everything."

"Lord, I'm trying to, but I feel miserable and I'm scared!
I'm hanging, barely hanging by an emotional thread. Paul
was a saint. He wrote in Philippians 'Your attitude should be
the same as that of Christ Jesus.' Oh, how I wish it could be,
right now!"

Then, to make me feel worse I read on in Philippians,
"Rejoice in the Lord always. Rejoice! Do not be anxious
about anything, and God's peace will guard your heart."

"Oh, Lord, I need some of your peace right now. I feel
so alone now and far from family. We don't even have any
close friends here in Morija whom I would ask to come and
pray with me about this. Oh, Lord! Help me now, I pray!"

Desperate for an answer, I rummaged through our collec-
tion of books and tapes. I found the tape that John and Patty
had given us years before from a pastor in England. As I read
over the label, I remembered that long trip we took to Ha
Sefako shortly after our arrival in Africa, how we had been
afraid when darkness fell on us, but how God had guided us
to their home. I recalled how the power of the Holy Spirit
was so evidently in their lives, and how nothing seemed to
ruffle them. They really were focused on the power of God.

I slipped the tape into the tape player and began to listen.
The pastor on the tape began to speak on the sin of pride.
He said that the reason that Christians don't move out in
the power of God is because there is too much pride in their
lives. It is by grace that we are saved and not of ourselves.

He was right! Here I was thinking more of myself than
anything else. I began to repent and weep.

The voice on the tape continued, "God only has good
gifts for us. Yes, He wants us all to be filled with the Holy
Ghost."

I listened raptly. He continued, "Many of us do not pray in tongues because of pride. We think it is of ourselves."

Again, I recalled how Charles and I had asked for the baptism of the Holy Spirit and were filled. We prayed and rejoiced, but when we shared it with Christian friends, they told us that it was not of God. We became quiet and no longer prayed in the Spirit.

I repented, crying out, "Lord, if this is what you want for us, a greater boldness in the Spirit, I want it! I will not turn back again! Please, Lord, I want confirmation that this is really of You. I want my family to see the difference in me first. And instead of praying in the spirit, I want to sing in an unknown tongue when I least expect it."

Yet, I still did not feel better. Suddenly a thought came to me. Not so long ago, a dear friend had written me a letter telling me of her prayers to be filled with the Holy Spirit to help her in her time of need. I, too, needed to ask the Holy Spirit to help me.

I cried out to God, "Oh Lord, I pray that the Holy Spirit will fill me so completely with His power and strength that there will be no room for nagging human thoughts and fears!"

As I continued to pray, fatigue overtook me and I fell into a deep, sound sleep. I did not awaken until I heard Barry and Tina's voices as they came home from school.

There was still that heavy feeling in my body, but I felt stronger and better physically.

Later that afternoon, a lady whom I had met shortly after coming to Morija came by just to visit. She had no idea that I had been sick. I shared with her what I would have to face. We prayed together about it. I know that God sent her to comfort me. After we prayed, she left, only to return about an hour later with another lady whom I hardly knew. They prayed with our whole family, and then helped us tuck Barry and Tina into bed. I could see the concern in Barry's eyes. I sat down on his bed and took his hand. He burst into tears. "Mom, I don't want you to go to the hospital!"

I just held him close to comfort him saying, "It's going to be okay. It's going to be okay…"

After Barry and Tina fell fast asleep these ladies prayed for Charles and me. They anointed my head with oil, praying for healing in my body. As they prayed, I became very expectant. I knew that God was touching me. As I began to praise Jesus, tears ran down my cheeks. A peace settled over me.

The next morning I awoke feeling so much lighter, and glad to be alive. I had slept so soundly the night before that I didn't even remember going to bed. I arose quickly because I knew I had to speak with Barry and Tina. We had arranged that they would stay with our neighbors who were missionaries from Switzerland.

I really prayed and asked the Holy Spirit to direct me in what to say to them. First, I told them how very much God loves us all and that there is no fear in love, and perfect love drives out fear. I explained to them that God loves us perfectly. I told them that every time I felt fear coming upon me, I would pray for them and every time they felt fear they could pray for me.

I said, "We must all three of us try to praise God and remember how much He loves us and cares for us. We must trust God."

Barry asked, "Mom, will they remove your breast?"

"Barry, honey, if my breast is diseased, it must go. But that's okay. We want our bodies to be perfect because our bodies are the temple of God. Remember the verse, 'Do not be afraid of those who kill the body but cannot kill the soul. Rather be afraid of the one who can destroy both soul and body in hell.'"

We prayed together. As they ran off to school, the thought crossed my mind, "Will I ever see them again?"

Then I said out loud, "I know that Barry and Tina are yours, Lord, and you love them much more than I do!"

I could not believe what was happening in my life. It was so powerful. It was the power of God!

George, Jim, Charles

Ed, Betty, Billy

Betty and Charles

Barry, Betty, Charles, Tina

Hospital Patient Lesotho

Feeding Program Lesotho

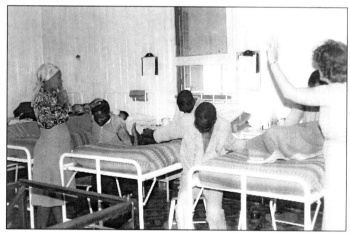

Hospital Ministry

Church Choir

Charles Mission Garage

Betty Leper Mission

Christian Revival Church, Ladybrand, South Africa

Charles Baptising

Our Grand-daughter Sharon, and Tina

Chapter 23

GOD'S GUIDANCE

Charles and I got in the car and headed for Bloemfontein, in South Africa, to see the doctor there. As Charles drove, I sat in the car reading my Bible, praying and praising God. Both of us were completely unaware of other problems brewing within the country.

We passed through Maseru and went straight to the border crossing. Since we frequently experienced delays there, we wanted to get there as early as possible in case there were any lines. However, we did not anticipate what we found. Usually when we arrive at the border we pay twenty cents and cross a long, single lane bridge for cars, trains, and people. That was not the case this particular morning.

Instead, waiting at the border was a line of cars that stretched back a couple of kilometers. And, the line was not moving. Cold and wet, hundreds of people huddled under blankets, blowing their fingers for warmth. Some had made fires from damp twigs, while others sat in their cars waiting.

I approached a man who was sitting in his car reading a newspaper, asking if he knew what the problem was. He showed me the headline of his paper which read, "BORDER TOWN BOTTLENECKED IN SOUTH AFRICAN POLICE

HUNT" in large bold type. He held it up long enough for me to read a lower headline which read, "PRETORIA BOMB TOLL NOW NINTEEN. SOUTH AFRICA MAY RETALIATE AGAINST BORDER STATES."

No one moved. We all just sat in our cars as the minutes passed. My doctor's appointment was scheduled for 11:00 A.M. and it was already 8:30. Bloemfontein was roughly 110 kilometers from Maseru and the road was good, so we had allowed ourselves plenty of time to get there. Now, I began to pray. I felt God leading me to walk across the bridge. I mentioned this to Charles and he agreed.

After passing all of the cars waiting in line at the border, I finally arrived at the gate. It was chained and locked with armed guards standing behind it. I explained to the guards that this was a medical emergency, showing the guards my papers. They led me into the administration building, taking me to a lieutenant who was supposed to help me.

He looked up at me. "May I see your papers?"

I gave them to him. He quickly perused them and affixed his signature.

"You're free to cross the border, but I don't know how you'll ever get your car through."

It didn't matter. To me, the most difficult step was accomplished.

Walking back to the Lesotho side of the border, I boldly walked up to the first car that was waiting and motioned to the driver to roll down the window. As he did, I told him, "This is a medical emergency. Can you back up and let our car through?"

I was surprised as he quickly pulled his car over to the side.

Before I got to the second car, the driver got out and said, "Let me help you, Madam."

He then proceeded to act as the traffic cop, and had all of the other cars pull out of the way. He ushered our car right to the front of the line. It took about an hour, but we were finally at the gate waiting for the car ahead of us to be searched. The search process took about an hour for every car. The lieutenant finally saw us waiting and waved us through without a search. We were on our way, praising God for his goodness and provision.

When we arrived in Bloemfontein, we found that the directions that the doctor in Morija had given us were clear and concise. We drove right to the specialist's office, about a half-hour late. There we found a note on the door written in Afrikaans. After a short search, we found someone to translate it for us. The note said that we must meet the doctor at the Universitas Hospital. We had no clue as to where it was or how to get there. The kind gentleman who interpreted the note agreed to take us there. We could clearly see that God was with us and helped us every step of the way.

We arrived at the hospital where we met the doctor. He began to examine me. After about ten minutes into the exam, he said to me, "I think I have good news for you."

"We've been praying that you would," I replied.

"Let me finish the exam, just to be sure, and I'll talk to you."

After finishing the exam, he explained, "What you have is a fibroid tumor. It is not malignant, nor is it dangerous. You should not worry."

He continued, "You must take care not to injure your breast, and wear good support. Also, I am writing instructions to your doctor to schedule a mammogram every three months for at least a year. We still need to keep a close watch on this."

He then was gracious enough to walk me down the corridor to meet Charles. I could read the concern on Charles' face as we entered the room. The doctor repeated to Charles that there was no sign of cancer. I fought back the tears as we hugged each other tightly, praising God.

After we left the hospital, we went to the home of some friends of our doctor from Morija. He had arranged for us to stay with them during our time in Bloemfontein. The first thing we did was call Barry and Tina to share the good news with them. The children were elated to hear it. They eagerly asked us when we were coming home. We told them that we would rest for a day and be home on Friday before they were home from school. We then had a sumptuous dinner, followed by tea.

As we drank tea with our new friends, Jacob commented, "Betty, you look so aglow, so radiant, and so full of the love of the Lord."

I couldn't believe my ears. I certainly didn't feel aglow. I was exhausted. Yet God was already answering my prayer. Others were seeing a 'difference' in me. I knew that God had really touched me.

The next day was wonderful. We rested, relaxed, and slept. The entire ordeal had taken its toll. I was exhausted, and I could tell that Charles, too, was tired. That extra day of rest was exactly what we needed

The next morning we arose at three and quietly left for Maseru. We wanted to get to the border early, in case we were delayed for an hour or so.

The road from Bloemfontein was practically deserted at that time of morning and the drive to the border took a little less than an hour. Charles and I felt more relaxed than we had been in weeks. However, at the border we discovered that instead of improving over the last few days, conditions had worsened. The line of vehicles waiting to cross the border was over a kilometer long. Resigning ourselves to several hours of waiting, we sat in the car; and sat; and sat; never moving.

The weather remained rainy and cold. Three hours passed. We didn't move, but we used the time productively for devotions, reading our Bible, praying, and praising God.

Finally, Charles got out of the car to see why no one was moving.

On down the line, he found a man who had been sitting in the line since about 5:00 p.m. on Wednesday. The day was now Friday. The man told Charles that he had moved only three car lengths in that time. We began to feel hopeless. By 2:00 that afternoon, we had become exhausted, cold, and hungry.

I suggested to Charles that we try the Riverside Lodge–right next to the border–for food, and perhaps, lodging. It was a difficult decision because we were afraid to lose our place in line. So we prayed. Some people said that if we left our car, maybe we could get through. We decided to try it.

Charles said to me, "Betty, you go into the lodge. This is South Africa and they will not want me in there. I'll stay out here in the car."

"Okay, honey. I'll try to get you a sandwich and bring it out here for you."

Inwardly, I prayed that the lodge management would let us stay, if necessary.

I entered the lodge and proceeded straight to the front desk. I found the clerk and asked, "I wonder if you can help me?"

"I'll be glad to help you," he replied. "Do you need a room?"

I nodded.

He hurried on, "That's no problem at all. We'll help you."

"There is a slight problem," I interrupted. "My husband is a black American."

With that he froze, the key in his hand, hanging in mid-air.

I heard a man's voice behind me speak with a British accent, "No, that should not be a problem."

I turned to see a white man speaking to the desk clerk rather authoritatively. He was an older man with white hair. I turned back to see the desk clerk looking at him oddly.

Just then a lady walked in. The tall Englishman turned and spoke to her. "Madeline, these Americans need a place to stay."

Then he moved closer and spoke to her quietly. I could not hear what he said to her, but she immediately reiterated to the desk clerk, "Of course, there is no problem. Please show these folks to their room."

I quickly thanked the Englishman and ran to get Charles at the car.

As I approached the car, he opened the door. "Well, what's the news?"

"We have a place to stay. They're letting us in."

"Did you tell them about me?"

"Of course I did. I'll tell you all about it, let's go."

As he carefully pulled up to the hotel, I explained the entire event. He just shook his head. "Praise God! He is always so faithful."

As we came in with our bags, ready to go to our room, the Englishman stopped us. He seemed concerned for us.

"Why do you need to get into Lesotho?"

"Well," I started, "we live in Morija, and our children are expecting us home this afternoon."

"Oh, I see. I thought you were just tourists."

"No, we are missionaries here and have been for five years now."

"Oh. Have you been waiting long?"

"We arrived here at five this morning," Charles answered.

"Hmm. That's bad."

Then he paused for a minute and continued, "You know, your car is probably the biggest hassle for getting across the border. If you need to get across, maybe you should try to leave your car parked here at the lodge and walk across."

We looked at each other thinking, "What a wonderful idea! Why didn't we think of that?"

We went to our room to pray about it. Then we tried to call Barry and Tina in Morija to explain our situation to them, but we could not get through. After some thought, we tried some friends in Maseru. That worked! They agreed to contact Barry and Tina and explain everything to them.

Filled with new hope, we agreed to try to walk across the bridge. As we headed to the border, hunger and fatigue were all but forgotten. After pushing our way through the crowd, we found the gate chained and locked with armed guards on duty.

I called out to one guard, "Sir, we are Americans, and we need to get back to our children. Can you help us?"

"Sorry, ma'am, the border is closed for today. Come back tomorrow morning at five."

"But isn't the border supposed to be open until ten tonight?"

"No. Not during these times, ma'am. Sorry."

Disappointed, we turned back, walking slowly to the lodge. I so wanted to hold Charles' hand, but we had learned not to be affectionate in public. We trudged on together, thankful that we had a nice warm place to stay.

After dinner we returned to our room to pray and praise the Lord. In short order we fell into a deep sleep until four the next morning.

We washed up quickly and had a good breakfast at the lodge, not knowing how long we would be waiting at the border. It was five in the morning and dark, foggy, damp, and very cold. Hundreds of miners, coming home for the weekend to visit their families in Lesotho, had arrived and were getting out of buses and into line. A guard finally came to the gate. We waited for him to open it, but he just stood there to guard it.

After a short while, I attracted his attention. "Sir, we need to get to Lesotho today."

I held up our visa. "We have only a four day medical emergency visa and it expires today. Can you help us?"

He looked at me blankly and asked, "Do you have a border pass? No one gets through the gate today without a border pass."

We did not have a border pass. We waited for another three hours with hundreds of miners pressing around us.

One of them asked, "Why will they not open the gates for us?"

I shrugged. I had no answer for them.

Finally another guard came. Again we tried to explain our desperate situation to him.

He just looked back and said flatly, "I can't help you."

After some time, our friend the Englishman strolled by, walking his dog. "Are you still here? I say, they are a bit obstinate today."

I nodded.

"Perhaps," he continued, "you should come back to the lodge. We can call the commander and explain your situation to him."

After a short prayer, we decided to stay at the border for a while longer. Soon another guard came to the gate. This was the same one to whom we had spoken the previous day.

I called to him, "Hey, remember us? We're still waiting."

He just looked back at us helplessly.

"Look," I said, "we were just here on an emergency medical visa and it expires today."

He took a look at it. Reluctantly he said, "Let me call my lieutenant. Perhaps he can help."

Again we waited, this time until noon. We finally saw him coming, but he turned to go elsewhere.

"Hey!" I called to him. "Can he help us?"

"Oh yeah! But not until Monday or Tuesday of next week."

More discouraged than ever, we finally gave in and returned to the lodge. As we came into the lobby of the lodge, we felt beaten and defeated. The manager was right there, and I'm sure she saw exactly how we were feeling.

Charles approached her. "Our English friend said that you could possibly help us?"

"I know Commander Briggs quite well. Let me call him."

We sat on a couch in the lobby while she called. At first, her face was friendly. We could tell that she was just exchanging pleasantries with him. The conversation went on and on. As it progressed, her face tightened, and she grew more and more frustrated.

Finally she hung up. I could tell she made no progress, but we still held a small grain of hope as she approached us.

"Well," she said, "it seems that no one will get through the border today. You may as well just relax and stay here."

In his quiet, but resolute manner, Charles said, "No! I'm getting through that border today! I'm going down there right now. Betty, you stay here."

By this time our English friend had joined us.

"Come, man. Let me go with you!"

As the two of them marched toward the border, I sat and prayed. I poured out my soul to the Lord as the psalmist said, "O God, do not keep silent. Be not quiet. O God, be not still. See how Your enemies are astir, how Your foes rear their heads. With cunning they conspire against Your people. They plot against those You cherish."

As I began to sing a song to the Lord, I noticed that I was singing in a different language, a language that I didn't know. God had answered my prayer. Suddenly, it was as if my whole being was full of the love of God. I knew that God was more than enough. I praised Him and worshipped Him and forgot the troubles of the border.

Suddenly our English friend burst through the door. "Mrs. McGee, Mrs. McGee, your husband got in. They are processing your papers right now. Come quickly!"

I leapt to my feet and dashed to the border with my friend following close behind. We pushed through the crowd to the locked gate. I called to the guard, "Sir, you've just let my husband in. Now I need to go with him."

He curtly spoke to me, "No way, Lady. I let no one through this gate without a border pass."

The Englishman was assertive but not rude. "Look Officer, I was with Mr. McGee when he came right up to you and you let him in. See, he's standing right over there. Now this is his wife and you must let her in!"

The guard looked at Charles. Then he looked back at us. Then he looked at the rest of the crowd, clamoring to get in. He did not say one word, but slowly opened the gate and I went in. After thanking our English friend, Charles took my hand and we walked across that long, narrow bridge. We thanked God for our new English friend whom the Lord had sent to help us.

When we got to the Lesotho side, a crowd had gathered, waiting for loved ones. When they saw us they broke out into cheers. They surrounded us, clapping and cheering as we came across. It was so good to be back in Lesotho! Two hours later we were back with our children, rejoicing in the Lord.

For the next few days, I rested. I had not completely recovered from the typhoid. One night, I awoke with an impulse to pray. I slipped out of bed so that I would not disturb my husband. After reading my Bible and praying, I felt God leading me to write down what had happened, and how He had moved so many mountains for us. I began to type. By the time I finished typing, it was nearly morning. I had been awake from one until five in the morning. But I felt so good! I knew that God was touching me in a way that I had never been touched before. I also knew that I was completely healed, even from typhoid.

As I prepared breakfast for my family, I continued to rejoice and sing praises unto the Lord.

Barry walked into the kitchen and put his arms around me. "Mommy, I want Jesus in my life!"

This confused me because Barry had accepted Jesus as his Savior a few months before.

"Barry, honey, I thought you made that decision a few months ago."

"Mommy, I want the new Jesus, like you have."

I stopped and held him close, praising God. Not only had God moved mountains for us, but I found myself giving thanks by singing in tongues when I least expected it. And... Barry, too, had noticed something 'different' in me. God was confirming His Word to me. God had already granted me the signs I had asked for. I found myself wondering what other adventures He had in store for us.

Chapter 24

FULL OF LOVE

With this very special experience with God, I felt like I was soaring! Just as Isaiah 40:31 says 'but those who hope in the Lord will renew their strength. They will soar on wings like eagles, they will run and not grow weary, they will walk and not be faint.' Something miraculous had happened to me on May 26th, 1983 and it changed me forever. God had poured His love out upon me in such a way that I had never experienced before.

I have no idea how or why this happened to me. All I remember is that I had felt so sick and I had been crying out to God for help. I had exhausted all of my own strength and was at the end of myself. I had felt so alone and so desperate! I also remember that when those people came to pray for me, I was hoping and expecting God to touch me and help me. At the time they prayed, I felt nothing.

Despite the horrific ordeal we had just been through, I knew God was doing a special work in my life. Everything seemed new to me and I felt so different. I felt such a peace – a real deep peace – it was God's peace within me. It was as though I knew, really knew 'My grace is sufficient for you, for my power is made perfect in weakness.'

I began to see everything differently–my husband, for instance. He was so full of compassion, love, understanding and wisdom. I saw the mighty man of faith and strength that God had given to me. It was almost as if God had opened my husband's entire being for me to see–and I liked what I saw. I watched our children with new eyes. They were so full of love, so innocent, so eager to learn and play and experience more of life. I even responded differently to what they said. I understood how richly God was blessing me and our family!

I read 'Whoever believes in me, as the scripture has said, streams of living water will flow from within him.' I felt like I was experiencing these streams of living water. These streams were flowing within me, and bubbling out and over. I just could not praise Him enough! One day, as I was praising God, I just threw my arms around myself and said "Thank you, Lord, for making me!" I was so in love with Him that I found I was beginning to love myself.

I also began to experience what Paul said: 'Pray without ceasing.' I found I was in continual communication with God and He with me. I would go to do something and all of a sudden I knew I should not do it; or I would go to say something and suddenly I knew I must remain quiet. I found myself praying or singing in tongues almost all of the time.

For the first time, I experienced the scripture 'Love not the world, neither the things that are in the world.' From my new perspective, the world and all the things of the world were around me, but nothing could touch me. I could see clearly that this was the way that God wanted me to live all of the time.

I found myself taking my Bible with me everywhere I went. I was looking into the Word at every opportunity. I could hardly get enough of it. It seemed that each time I opened the book His word spoke to me in a unique and precious way. Every word became a blessing. I would now spend hours meditating on one scripture. Each afternoon I would spend two or three hours just reading the Word and talking to Jesus, my Lord.

It is written in Psalm 37:4 'Delight thyself in the Lord and He shall give thee the desires of thine heart.' Truly God had done that for me. He filled me with Himself. My spirit now communed with the Spirit of God in this total immersion of the Baptism of the Holy Spirit. I was no longer ruled by my mind, my will or my emotions. My 'spirit man' had been separated from my emotions and from my flesh. I was no longer subject to the thoughts of fear or depression and anxiety. Those emotions became subject to my inner man who is in perfect communion with the Spirit of God. When my spirit prays, I am praying the perfect will of God according to the scriptures. When I don't know what to pray for or how to pray, the Spirit himself intercedes for me. The scriptures say that is giving thanks well and praying in my most holy faith. Praise God. My inner man knows that I am His and it fills me with such joy I cannot express it. He, my God, my Savior, has given me the greatest desire of my heart – Himself!

Not only was God working in my life and in our home, but He was also touching all of us in a dynamic way. We spent even more time praying and praising. One day Barry leapt into his father's arms and said, "Jesus took my tongue." Our children began singing and praising God in their new heavenly language. We found we had an unquenchable desire to come closer and closer to God.

This inexpressible love of God continued in me for many months and changed our lives dramatically. We found we were growing bolder, stronger and we were hungry to serve others.

The passion of God's love filled me once again. Yes, God had touched me in a very special way and filled me to overflowing with His love. I found myself wondering, why me Lord? I'm nothing special. He loves us so much. I felt a new confidence rising up within me.

Chapter 25

BOLD AS A LION

As the signs of war continued all around me, a thought came to me. Maybe I could try to leave just before dawn tomorrow morning. I had noticed at that time of morning the sounds of battle were less intense.

I wondered if the American Embassy could even help me. Had their plan with the special troops succeeded in evacuating people? They said they would contact me again. Should I wait for them to call? No, if this is as bad as everyone says, maybe I should make my own plans.

I think I'm bold enough to try it on my own. I remembered another bold act.

We felt compelled, as a family, to go to the streets of Maseru and preach the gospel. We did not get on a soap box and start shouting to the masses, but instead we approached individuals with a leaflet and told them about Jesus' love. One of the first people that we met was Me' Mathabo. Already a Christian, she was very motivated and eager to help us. That is how she became our interpreter. Within the first two weeks there were about thirty people who got saved and were eager to know more about the Lord. The next step was to get them into a good strong church so they could grow in their walk with the Lord.

We approached several pastors from local established churches, sharing with them what we were doing, and asking if they would take these people into their churches. Because of our language deficiencies, we felt that it would be better for their spiritual growth to be in churches guided by people who spoke Sesotho. The pastors all received us warmly and said they would be more than happy to take these people in. After that, whenever a person with whom we spoke made a profession of faith, we would refer them to a church, depending upon where they lived.

Then, the bad news reached us. People met us on the streets to tell us that the churches we sent them to preached that we were a cult.

I suppose the pastors from these churches spoke to each other about us. They actually warned their congregations to have nothing to do with us. And, worst of all - they did not want the people that we sent to them.

How sad and disappointed this made us. But, we had responsibilities. We were not prepared to start a church, but these people needed a place to help them in their walk with the Lord.

We prayed. There was no mistake that God was leading us to look after these people, at least for right now. They really needed to be discipled.

And so began our first church.

Chapter 26

CHURCH PLANTING

To look after and help these new Christians in their walk with the Lord, we needed a place to gather. Since we were now living in Morija, it was impractical to use our home. It was much too far away. We decided to approach our friends, Blaine and Marian Fosse. They were both from the United States. Blaine was an engineer with the U.S. government involved in a water reclamation project in Lesotho. They had both been to our prayer meetings when we lived in Lithabaneng. It was during that time that Marian received the Lord and became born again. When we approached them about using their house, they not only consented, but were very excited about it.

We now had a place to meet. Betty led the praise and worship with her guitar while I preached and Me' Mathabo translated. We continued to go to the streets every Saturday and share the Word of God with anyone who would listen. Within a matter of weeks, the Fosse house became much too small to hold the people. After much prayer we were able to find an old movie theater that we could rent for Sunday mornings. Within a few months, our congregation blossomed into 150 members.

Although the church was growing exponentially, we knew that it would be limited if we continued in the leadership positions. It was crucial to the survival of the church that we find some local Mosotho man to take over the pastorate. With our language challenges, our ability to truly minister to the people was handicapped. Furthermore, we knew that as Americans we would one day return to America, leaving the work behind to someone else. So we began to pray about the situation, passionately and fervently.

One evening the phone at our house rang. It was Jacob, a white man from South Africa whom we had met on a previous occasion. He asked if he could attend our services on the following Sunday. Not wanting to turn anyone away, we readily consented.

Jacob had been spending some time with a friend of his, Pastor Crew from Pretoria. The Pastor had asked Jacob what he knew about us. Apparently the senior pastor from Hatfield Christian Church had heard about our work in Maseru and wanted to meet with us. So Jacob came to our church for a visit and invited us to come to Pretoria in a few weeks to visit with him and Pastor Crew.

At this very fruitful meeting the first thing that Pastor Crew asked was, "What does your church need more than anything?"

Without hesitation I replied, "We need a local man to pastor this work."

"Well, that's the one thing that I really can't help you with. We have people in our church that could pastor on a temporary basis, but I don't think that's what you need. Our people probably wouldn't do as well as you have. All I can offer on that front is to agree with you in prayer."

"That would be marvelous."

"We could send an evangelism team a couple of times a year to help out."

"That would be wonderful!"

After spending some time with them, we left for home, knowing that the Lord had provided a wonderful covering for our ministry in Maseru.

One of the most faithful ladies in the church was our translator, Me' Mathabo. She, like many of the women of Maseru, had a husband who worked in the mines of South Africa. His name was Ntate Dickson. The mine where he worked was located near Welkom, a city about 100 kilometers north of Maseru. Since the distance was not too great, Ntate Dickson was able to come home once a month, unlike many men who were only able to make it back two or three times a year. And he was faithful to come home on a regular basis. Whenever he came home, he would always come to church, so we would see him once a month.

The more we came to know Me' Mathabo and Ntate Dickson, the more we were impressed with the way they walked with the Lord and were truly sincere in their faith. We learned that during his evenings at Welkom Ntate Dickson had gone to Bible College and graduated with honors. It soon became apparent to us that this young man would become the pastor of the church. We felt he was the local leader that God was raising up. We knew that God would confirm this by speaking to him about it.

It was about six months later that he came to us in tears, saying that he had not been obedient to the Lord and His call on his life. So we began to pray with him. After a great deal of prayer and seeking God's guidance, and hearing from Him, we began to work very closely together with Ntate Dickson and his wife. It was such a privilege to see God working so mightily in their lives.

Frequently, we visited Pastor Crew in Pretoria to discuss the work of the church. Each time Ntate Dickson would come with us, because he knew in his heart that God was calling him to pastor this church. It took a great step of faith on his part because he made good money at the mines and he and Me Mathabo had two beautiful children to raise and provide for.

But God had a plan from the start. The people at Hatfield Christian Church in Pretoria offered to pay his salary for three years until the church could become self-supporting. We continually see God's hand of provision when we hear His voice and obey Him.

We always took our concerns to God in prayer, even to the naming of the church. We called the church, Zoë Bible Church, (meaning the Love of God). During those first years we experienced so much of God's grace and many other blessings.

We continued to go to the streets of Maseru every Saturday. It was just a part of life for all of us. Barry and Tina always came with us. As we witnessed to people, we saw miraculous things begin to happen.

One day as we spoke, one lady in particular seemed very interested and eager to receive Jesus Christ as her savior. We both gave our personal testimonies and prayed with her. We could see her light up as she received Jesus into her life. As we continued to share together, we discovered that this woman was a prostitute.

She looked to us with pleading eyes and said, "I have a man coming to me tonight. What must I do when he comes?"

With no hesitation we told her, "God is more than enough. You are a new creation in Him now. He will show you what to do."

We continued to pray for her. We knew that God would provide for her and show her the way.

The next morning we went back to Maseru for church in the movie theater. Betty led praise and worship and I gave the Word of God. The power of God was present to heal and save and many were touched by God. As soon as the service was dismissed, that young lady we had prayed with yesterday rushed to the front of the church to share with us her experience from the night before.

She started, "I went home, full of the joy of the Lord, singing and worshipping my new Savior. It was like I wanted to burst. Yet, I had to prepare for this man who would come to me that night. As I prepared, I kept singing praises to the Lord, hoping that the man would not come. However, before I was ready, he was at my door. He was a regular, so he was eager to see me. When he came in and we faced each other, he began to tremble all over. He had not even touched me and he began shaking like a leaf. Then he reached into his pocket, pulled out the amount of money he always paid me, threw the money on my bed, and ran out of my house without a word. I knew that I knew that I knew that Jesus had set me free in every area. I've never been so happy."

We rejoiced in the goodness and faithfulness of God. More and more, people were saved and healed as this church grew into a congregation of over 3,000 people. We did what we felt led to do, and just watched the growth as God continued to pour His Spirit out upon this thirsty land.

Chapter 27

MORE BLESSINGS

After living in Lesotho for over six years and managing the Morija garage for over two years, I could see some of the fruits of my labor. I felt that maybe I had someone capable of taking over for a couple of months. Pastor Dickson and Me' Mathabo could take care of the church. Since Betty was home schooling Barry and Tina, travel was not an issue and we decided to take a home leave. We made plans to be away in June and July so we could be away for most of the winter in Lesotho and be in the United States during the summer. It was a small way we indulged ourselves.

We returned home to visit our families in June of 1985 with financial support issues on our minds. M.C.C. only worked with three-year contracts, and we had already renewed once. We could no longer expect to receive support from M.C.C..

We always took our concerns to the Lord in prayer. God seemed to say, 'Keep your eyes on me, keep trusting me, I am more than enough'. We refused to worry about it. Our friends from the Lesotho Evangelical Church did not want us to leave, either. Before we left on leave, they sent someone to tell us that they would be seeking support for us while we were away.

We took a two-month leave and did many of the same things that we had done on our previous leave. My mother was in pretty good health for a lady in her 80's. Betty's mother was still doing well and living in St. Louis with Betty's brother, Ed.

During our second week back in the States, we took Tina to Springfield to be tested by a specialist there. We wanted to know why she was struggling in certain areas.

The appointment was for 11:00 that Monday morning. We spent Sunday night with my brother, Bill, and his wife, Connie. Their children, Derek and Angela, were about the same age as Barry and Tina. We all had a really great time together.

We stayed up late that night, sharing together and catching up. Bill and Connie had many questions about home schooling. They mentioned that some teachers were a little skeptical about home-schooling. They wanted to know if their children could really benefit from such a thing. We assured them that Barry and Tina had plenty of time with people of their own age. And, Betty was able to give more attention to Tina with her special problems to make sure that she learned. (Interestingly enough, both Bill and Connie eventually left the teaching profession and began to home school their children.)

The next morning we took Tina to the specialist. After about an hour in the examination room, Tina came out, followed by the doctor.

He spoke gently, "Now, Tina, you stay here for a few minutes. I need to talk to your mom and dad."

He motioned us into his office.

Closing the door behind us he started, "I'm afraid your daughter has extreme dyslexia. It will take hard work to overcome it."

"Well," Betty asked, "what do we do?"

"First I'd suggest that she be taught orally as much as possible. She's fallen behind a little in school, so she should be able to catch up that way. She is a bright girl."

"Okay, we can handle that. Is there a cure for it?"

"Actually, no. But with proper instruction and a lot of hard work, Tina can learn to read and function normally in society."

"Okay, we'll help her all we can."

"That brings me to the next issue. I really believe that you should rethink your plans to return to Africa. Being in that environment would probably do too much damage to her emotionally."

"What do you mean?" I wondered out loud.

"She just needs to be in a place where there are the resources to help her. I think that if she continues to fall behind, her self-esteem will suffer."

This was unexpected. We weren't prepared to deal with the problem from this perspective. Betty and I said nothing for what seemed like forever.

Finally I said, "We'll pray about it."

We left and went back to St. Louis to spend a few more days with Betty's mother. During that time, when Betty and I were alone, we spent quite a bit of time discussing the situation about Tina. Every day and night we prayed asking God what He wanted us to do. Each time we prayed, we sensed that God continued to say, 'Trust Me, I know your needs.' We knew in our hearts that we must return to Africa. Perhaps the doctor did not understand our environment or the resources that were possibly available to us in Lesotho. We had peace about returning to Africa and we knew that God had a very special plan for us.

While in St. Louis, we received a call from the pastor at our old church in Kitchener. He said that the mission office wanted to speak to us. This struck us as odd since we had gone overseas with a volunteer mission group and were considered "missionaries on loan" by our own church, but we agreed to meet with them. We had never even applied with our own mission board to go overseas. I kept wondering why they wanted to see us.

We felt a little bit intimidated, walking into a big room and seeing twelve men sitting at a long table. But, they were cordial enough as we were introduced and invited us to sit at the head of the table. After some small talk, they began to ask us questions about our work in South Africa. As we began to talk about what God was doing in South Africa, we saw how receptive these men were to our story. They asked about our work, our living conditions, and the people around us. When we shared about play day and our visits to the leper mission, more than one eye began to tear.

As the group continued to ask questions, we talked about the planting of Zoë Bible Church in Maseru and how Pastor Dickson was growing into a wonderful leader. As the meeting concluded, I looked at my watch and noticed that almost two hours had passed. Before we left, they asked if they could pray for us. They all gathered around us, laid their hands on us and prayed for God's Spirit to be on us continually, and for Him to bless our work in Lesotho.

We left the meeting still wondering why they had called us there, but grateful for the time of sharing together with them.

We really enjoyed our home leave with family and friends but it was time for us to return again to Lesotho. It was about two hours before we were to leave for the airport. The doorbell rang. It was a telegram for us from Lesotho. It read, "Do not return to Lesotho. We have not been able to raise any support. We repeat, do not return to Lesotho." I looked at Betty and said, "Let's pray." As we were praying and asking God for clear direction in our lives, again, the doorbell rang.

We were really surprised to see our dear friends from Lestowel, Ontario who had come to say goodbye before we left. I was so glad to see them. I handed the telegram to Bill and said, "You're just in time to pray with us for God's direction." Bill read it, smiled great big and handed it back to me, as he said, "This is not from God. This is from man. You already know what God has told you to do." We all laughed together and threw the telegram away. We praised the Lord and prayed and rejoiced together and off we went to the airport. We knew that God wanted us to return to Africa and He would take care of us there.

We arrived in Lesotho three days later and our missionary friends collected us at the airport. They were so glad that we had returned. They feared that if we got that telegram that we might not return. We shared with them that God was in control and we were trusting Him in every area. They shared with us that maybe their mission in Switzerland would consider supporting us. And, their director of Missions was in Lesotho now and wanted to interview us. We were interviewed and accepted the very next day. God is always so faithful.

On Monday, I returned to work only to discover a problem. At the garage, the first thing I did was look at the books to see how the garage had done during my absence. It didn't take long to see that something was awry. I had taken an inventory of all parts in stock before leaving. When I returned I found a great deal of inventory missing.

I left Wilson Mosili in charge. I had felt that Wilson was a good enough mechanic and manager to keep the garage going for awhile.

On the afternoon of that first day, I called Wilson into my office. "Close the door, Wilson."

"Ntate Charles, you find everything okay?"

"Well, not really. I have R10,000 worth of parts missing. I left you in charge. Can you account for them?"

He began to stammer, "I…I…"

"You stole them, didn't you?"

Looking at the ground he muttered, "How did you know so soon? Who told you?"

"No one told me, Wilson. I count these parts regularly. It didn't take much to realize that something was wrong. Why would you do this and put your job at risk?"

Wilson could see that I knew the truth.

I continued, "It will take time, but we will make it up. However, you will probably never have an opportunity like this again. If I cannot trust you, you cannot work for me. Take your things and leave."

Wilson left and never came back. He was probably relieved that I did not press charges against him. The rest of the mechanics in the shop took note. After that, I always tried to observe the integrity level of my employees, as well as their desire and ability to learn.

At home, we continued to pray about Tina and the dyslexia. Betty contacted Maseru Prep, where Tina and Barry had gone to school while we lived in Lithabaneng. To Betty's amazement, she discovered that the school had just hired a teacher who was trained as a specialist in dyslexia. Betty felt this was God's confirmation that He wanted us back in Africa. After an interview with Tina, the special teacher expressed a desire to teach her at Maseru Prep. Barry was pleased to be enrolled at Machabeng Secondary School, which was right next to Maseru Prep.

We were able to arrange for Betty to housesit for several people in Maseru during this time so that she could be with the children during the week. They would come back to Morija to spend the weekends at home with me.

A few weeks later, we received a letter from the Missionary Church of Canada.

It read:

Dear Mr. & Mrs. McGee:

Thank you so much for taking time during your home leave to visit with us and our mission board. We enjoyed our time immensely.

As a result of our visit together, the board has decided to license you both as pastors in our church. We realize that licensing will in no way enhance your spiritual walk, but we hope that it will lend you some credibility and help you in the church you have so successfully started there. The licenses will be arriving under separate cover within a few weeks.

Thank you so much for your witness and we will continue to pray that God will continue to bless your work abundantly.

Sincerely:
The Mission Board

This was amazing. We were not thinking or looking for this, or any other kind of recognition, nor did we feel that we needed it. It was a blessing from God.

About three weeks later we received our licenses. A few days later we received a note from a pastor friend of ours who had been at the meetings where they had voted to license us. He said that the vote was unanimous, and that Betty was the first woman to be licensed as a pastor in the Missionary Church.

Barry and Tina continued to go to school in Maseru for the next year. Tina began catching up nicely and she loved her teacher. Barry was an honors student. God continued to provide for us in every way.

On my way home from work one afternoon I stopped at the post office and found a letter from the Switzerland Mission. I decided to read it at home. Betty was reading it with me. It said, 'Due to a lack of funds in our Mission account we can no longer support you. Your support has been dropped, effective immediately. We are sorry we could not give you more notice.' I could not believe it! I silently prayed, 'Lord, we really need another Word from you now.' I flopped down on the sofa and continued praying. Our Bible was lying on the coffee table and it was open. I picked it up and my eyes fell on Heb 13:5 (Amplified) 'I will not in any way fail you nor give you up nor leave you without support, I will not, I will not, I will not in any degree leave you helpless nor forsake you, nor let you down nor relax my hold on you, assuredly not!' I was excited. I read this out loud to Betty. I took her hand and we prayed and thank God that He was assuring us that He is our source, all the time.

We told no one that we were without support from a mission or from a church. We just kept our eyes on Jesus. It was really amazing. Money kept coming to us, from sources we would never have thought of. If we needed school uniforms, the money was there. We had more coming into us than ever before. We did not lack in any area. God was so faithful to us. We were continually amazed at His constant goodness to us and His perfect timing in every area. One day groceries were short, our fridge was empty and a lady walked in with bags of groceries for us. This went on for four or five years. Money even came in for another home leave.

We took our home leave and while on this leave, the Church in Canada contacted us again and they interviewed us again and prayed with us again and asked all kinds of questions again about our work. Upon our return to Lesotho we got a letter from World Partners and they wanted to support us, starting immediately (as a result of our meeting with the Church in Canada). We had never asked for this. God was showing Himself strong on our behalf.

Thinking back on these many blessings from God I was beginning to see clearly again that He cares about every single detail of our lives. I felt confident, now more than ever, that He was giving me my plan of escape and that He would be with me every minute, guiding me and protecting me.

Chapter 28

LIVING BY FAITH

I desperately wanted to hear that Charles was safely out of Maseru. But, I knew that sitting here thinking about it would not help. Since we were leaving early tomorrow, Tina and I decided to do some last minute shopping. Even during war, life goes on.

We wanted to get a few more things for Barry's new town home. Although we did not have a lot to spend, we knew God would help us just as He always had.

We remained deeply involved in our work at Zoë Bible Church, which continued to grow steadily. Pastor Dickson and Me' Mathabo were wonderful leaders. During this time we would take trips to Bloemfontein about three or four times per year. Usually, we brought several other pastors with us. That little red Peugeot would get pretty crowded. As a result, we would sometimes have to leave someone behind.

Charles and I began to think that it would be nice to have a Kombie (van). As was our custom, we began to pray about it.

Since Charles was the mechanic for the Lesotho Evangelical Church and the one who managed their garage, he also became the designated car buyer. Whenever the church needed to purchase a new car, they would send Charles to Bloemfontein to pick it up at a Toyota dealership there. Over the years, Charles became pretty good friends with one of the sales representatives. Nico was truly a professional, and very honest. He always spoke to Charles with great admiration and respect, not as the average South African white man would speak to a black man.

Frequently, Charles went to Bloemfontein for parts. On these trips, he would occasionally stop in to visit with Nico. Those visits always proved an enjoyable way to keep up on what was developing in the automotive industry.

During one of those visits, Charles mentioned how we needed a Kombie for our work. He told Nico that someday we were going to get one. We couldn't get one yet because we only had R10,000 and the Kombie that we needed was R27,000.

Nico asked Charles what kind of Hi-Ace we had in mind. Charles dreamily picked out a color and then found that the one he really wanted came with a gaudy bright orange stripe. Charles asked about that and Nico told him that model came with the stripe, no other way. He was disappointed.

About four weeks later, the phone rang and Charles answered.

"Hello, Charles?"

"Yes?"

"Charles, this is Nico from Orange Toyota."

"Oh! Hi, how are you doing?"

"I have that Toyota Hi-Ace for you. The exact one you wanted!"

Charles became silent, not quite knowing what to say. Finally he protested, "What do you mean? I didn't order a vehicle from you."

"Ah, but you said you needed one, didn't you?"

"Yes, but I also told you I didn't have the money for it. Remember, I said someday."

"Well, you need to come over tomorrow to look at it. See you then."

Charles hung up the phone, stunned. He turned to me and told me what happened.

That night before we went to bed, we prayed about it. God seemed to be saying to us, "I am more than enough." So we decided to take the kids and go and look at it the next day.

That night I had a dream. We were in Nico's office talking about the Hi-Ace. He handed the keys to Charles and said, "Take it home, Charles. It's yours. Pay me whenever you can. Now, go on! Get out of here!"

I awoke quickly. The dream seemed so real. I woke Charles and told him all about it.

"That's nice, Betty, but that could never happen. Once that car gets into Lesotho, they could never get any money for it. They are separate countries. A South African man would never take that kind of a chance."

We prayed again and went back to sleep.

The next morning, all four of us piled into the church truck and drove to Bloemfontein. When we walked into Orange Toyota I was stunned. It was just like what I saw in my dream. Charles introduced us and we sat down with Nico and talked about the Hi-Ace.

The first thing he said was, "Well, go out and look it over."

We looked at it longingly. It was beautiful, and exactly what we needed; and it was brand new! The most amazing thing was that this Hi-Ace did not have that orange gaudy stripe. How could this be?

When we returned to Nico's office, Charles said. "It's really nice. When we get the money, we'll definitely consider it. Tell me, why doesn't it have that ugly orange stripe?

Nico said, "I don't know, that's a first." Then he looked at Charles and held up the keys. "Take it home, Charles, and you can pay me whenever you have the money."

We just stood there with our mouths gaping. We were in shock.

He said, "I know you'll pay me when you can, Charles. Now, go on, get out of here. I have work to do."

Charles slowly took the keys from his hand. Charles began to thank him for trusting us.

Nico interrupted him, "Goodbye, Charles. I'll see you next week."

I drove the Hi-Ace home and Charles took the church truck. Of course, the kids had to ride in the new car. When we finally arrived home, we all piled into the Hi-Ace and dedicated it to the Lord and to His work. God's grace and providence amazed us once again.

We knew God had chosen the perfect Hi-Ace for us and now we could trust him for the money to pay for it. We found the scripture in Philippians 4:19 that said "But my God shall supply all your need according to His riches in glory by Christ Jesus." We printed the scripture in big bold letters and hung it on the wall just outside of the kitchen. We agreed that every time we passed the scripture we would touch it and praise God for the money that He provided to pay for the Hi-Ace. We didn't quote the word every day, but we touched it and thanked God for the money every day and sometimes even two to three times a day.

One week passed, and there was no money. Another week, nothing. During our next Wednesday night prayer meeting about twenty-five people had joined us at our home. I felt led to praise God for the Hi-Ace and the money to pay for it. I began to get lost in praise of the Lord. Then everyone joined us, praising God for nearly an hour. After the meeting everyone congratulated us for getting the money to pay for the Hi-Ace. We just nodded and thanked them. We never told them that the money was not yet there.

The next morning, a letter arrived in the mail from very special friends who were not even a part of our church.

We found a check enclosed for even more money than we needed for the Hi-Ace. They said that they had just received an inheritance and felt led to bless us. The four of us knelt down together, held hands, and praised God for His goodness to us. His timing was perfect.

The following week, all four of us went to Bloemfontein, walked into Nico's office and paid the full R27,000 for the Hi-Ace. Nico took the money and said, "I really wasn't worried about it at all. I knew you would pay me for it. I hope you're enjoying it."

Once again, we faced the challenge of school for Barry and Tina. I considered going back to home schooling them. This time I looked into getting certified through ACE (Accelerated Christian Education). While I was looking into the program, several of our minister friends talked to us about a new interracial Christian school that would be opening the following term in Bethlehem, South Africa. They all seemed pretty excited about it, so we decided to investigate. We knew the pastor who was going to assume the headmaster position, and were really fond of him.

On several occasions we went to visit the pastor to talk about what the school was to be about. It seemed like an excellent idea, so we signed the children up for the school. Barry and Tina were not too sure about this new school idea. Barry's voice was beginning to change, and he was beginning to look more like a man than a young boy. He was stocky and muscular.

Tina was still a little shy, but just a delight to be with. She had truly benefited from her year at Maseru Prep with the help of her special teacher. Charles and I were excited to have them start at this new school.

About a week before school was to start, we were disappointed to find out that our pastor friend had resigned and would be leaving the area. I was not very happy about that but we were assured by others that everything would go on as planned. We also knew the senior pastor at the school and loved and respected him. He told us another man was moving in as headmaster of the school.

When we arrived with the children for the first day of school, we were greeted by the new headmaster. He seemed to be nice enough, so we settled Barry and Tina into their dorm rooms and went back to Morija.

Each weekend we would go and collect them. It was about a three-hour trip there and back, but it was well worth it. I would leave early Friday afternoon, and then we would take them back on Sunday evening.

In only a few weeks, however, I sensed something was wrong. I kept hearing the word "kaffer" from Barry and Tina. "Kaffer" is a derogatory term for a black person in South Africa. When I asked them where they had heard it, they told me that their classmates used it.

I never heard the full story until much later. But this is what took place:

Some of the older boys had been teasing Tina, calling her a kaffer. One day, Barry happened to be near and overheard it going on. He grabbed the one young man by the shirt collar, lifting him up off the ground and pinned his body against the building, as he said, "Are you going to call me a kaffer, too?"

The young man, full of fear, shook his head. Barry put him down. Needless to say, Barry was disciplined for the incident. The young man was not corrected in any way.

Barry and Tina never volunteered any information about any of these incidents. Even at their age they felt duty-bound to make the most of the situation, much as they had seen us doing it as a family through the years. After about six weeks of uneasiness, I decided to go and spend the weekend with them at the school. There was a presentation at the church on Friday night, so it was a good excuse for me to stay there.

As I sent them off to the presentation, I touched Barry's face with a quick, gentle caress. He winced as I drew my hand back. There on the right side of his face was a small scratch that I had apparently made with my diamond ring.

Instinctively, he looked at my ring and said, "Look, Mom, one of your diamonds is gone from your ring. Do you want us to look for it?"

I looked, and sure enough, not the main diamond, but a tiny little diamond had indeed fallen out of its setting in my ring and was lost. I said, Barry, I wouldn't know where to begin to look, just leave it."

As I sat through this church meeting, I just didn't feel right about something. I was also angry that I had lost that diamond from the ring Charles had given me so many years before. I found myself saying, 'Satan, you're a liar and a thief, but you will not get by with this.' I began to pray, 'Lord, I just don't feel right about all of this. There's a problem here. Help me and give me special wisdom, I pray.' Suddenly an idea came to me. So I continued to pray, 'Lord, if I am right (that something is wrong here) then I want You to lead me to the diamond that fell out of my ring.' I began to relax and enjoy the rest of the service.

To find a diamond that minute would be nearly impossible. I had no idea where I had lost it or when, and it was so small. I didn't seriously search for it, because I had already talked to God about it. I did feel around in my bed and around and under my pillow. Neither did I tell Barry or Tina about my talk with God about it.

The next morning I wanted to put a few things into the Hi-Ace, so I said to Barry, "Barry, could you back the Hi-Ace up to the door so that I don't have to carry these things so far?"

"Sure, Mom."

As he started to climb in to get behind the wheel, he cried, "Mom, Mom, come look."

I ran up to him to see that when he opened the door, that tiny diamond was right under the clutch of the car, brilliantly reflecting the morning sunlight. It was at the perfect angle to catch the sun's rays. I looked to the sky and said, "Thank you, Lord for your goodness and your confirmation."

I went to the senior pastor of the church, with whom both Charles and I were very close. I said to him, "Something's wrong here that I just can't put my finger on. And as far as I'm concerned, the Lord has just confirmed it, so I'll be taking Barry and Tina out of school today. They will not be coming back."

He looked at me in a strange sort of way, and then said, "I understand. You do what you must do."

After I left his office, I immediately called Charles and told him what I had done. He said that he, too, had been praying about it and thought that it was the right thing to do.

Then I told Barry and Tina. They were elated. After we returned home, they disclosed a lot more about the school. And, within months, we heard that the other pastor had also resigned and moved on.

We continued to pray about schooling for our children. Some of our missionary friends suggested Treveton. Apparently Treverton was a very good boarding school located on the Mooi River, near Durbin. It was completely on the other side of Lesotho. At Treverton, both children thrived. Barry begged the headmaster to allow him to enter high school, but the headmaster felt that because it was his first year at the new school he should be put back a year. He felt it would be better all around.

Barry was upset, so he talked to his dad about it. Charles scheduled a conference with the headmaster. During the conference there was a great deal of "head butting" and arguing about it. No one would budge from their position. Charles was sure that if Barry weren't challenged he would be getting into mischief and creating problems. The headmaster was certain that Barry could not keep up because this was a very 'tough' school.

Finally the headmaster looked Charles in the eye and said, "I'll put him into high school, but I'll guarantee you that I'll be putting him back in a month."

Charles answered, "Sir, if he doesn't make it, I will come back here and put him back, myself. I'll save you that job."

"Okay, you have a deal."

So Barry was excited about starting into their high school program.

About six weeks later we received a letter of apology from the headmaster admitting that he was mistaken. Barry was making straight A's. He was also very good and very popular in sports.

Tina also thrived in Treverton. They were equipped to deal with her dyslexia. She learned well and became quite proficient in swimming. She also developed wonderful people skills. She was made the lead person in charge of her dormitory and when they had to leave Treverton, most of the girls cried.

We had finally found a place where we didn't have to worry about our children's education. Unfortunately, it only lasted a little over a year.

Tina and I had a wonderful time shopping together. I realized how blessed and grateful to God I am for our children. What a joy to spend time with them! What a comfort it is to pray together with them for Charles!

Chapter 29

CRIME AND TRAGEDY

M id-day and the sky was black. The acidic smell of smoke burned my eyes and throat. How long would this go on, and could I hold out until morning to accomplish my plan?

Lord give me the strength to hold on until day break. You've never let me down and You are all I've got to hold onto now, help me Lord, I pray.

I kept praying and praising and found my mind beginning to think of God's past faithfulness in my life.

In the mid 1980's, political unrest continued to be normal. Chief Leabua Jonathan remained the prime minister of the country at the time. Several members of the ANC had taken refuge in Lesotho from the South African government. Chief Jonathan had given them asylum and refused to give them up. In response, the South African government set up a blockade around the borders of Lesotho. This created greater unrest since Lesotho was totally dependent on South Africa economically. Nothing could get in or out of Lesotho. In January of 1986, Major-General Justin Metsing Lekhanya seized power in a bloodless coup and made several political moves, including sending the ANC refugees back to South

Africa. Although it made many unhappy, the borders were again opened and business continued in Lesotho.

One of the consequences of the unrest was a rise in crime. Burglaries, muggings, and robberies went on virtually unchecked. Even our home was burglarized several times. We were blessed by God's protection. One time we were house sitting for another missionary family in Maseru, and we had uninvited visitors.

On that evening we were all very tired so we went to bed at about eight o'clock. The house had bare wooden floors and long hallways. We were staying in this house to look after their dog. The dog chose to sleep under our bed. At about one in the morning, I was disturbed from a deep sleep by the opening of our bedroom door.

I sat up quickly, thinking it was Barry.

With that I heard feet running down the hall. I jumped out of bed to pursue the footsteps, with Betty right behind. I saw four men running for the back door. Barry and Tina awoke to all of the commotion. The four men escaped with school bags, clothing, luggage, and many other valuables. We noticed the dog was still sleeping under the bed.

We quickly phoned the police, but to no avail. Someone did come out and take the report, but the best that we could get was that we were "lucky" that we were not killed when we encountered them. The officer told us that most people were either stabbed or shot during such an encounter.

On Sundays, we usually left for church at about 9 a.m. and would usually get home after 4 p.m. in the afternoon. At this time, we had a very large, very vicious dog. We were always careful to keep her chained when we were gone, so she would not injure anyone. After our return home one Sunday, our neighbor came over to our car and told us that our dog had been barking. They noticed one of our windows was wide open, but they had seen nothing else. This was not a good sign.

When we got into the house we knew we had been robbed. Our radio was gone and Barry and Tina's suitcases, packed and ready for school, were also gone. Barry ran to see the dog. She was still barking furiously. He unchained her and she immediately charged the fence, trying to get out. Barry was so excited.

He said to me, "Dad, let me put a chain on Pepper and we'll try to find the robbers."

Betty immediately said, "No! If you find them they may attack you, or even try to kill you."

I agreed, "No Barry, it's too dangerous."

The dog kept charging the gate and barking fiercely. Barry kept begging me. Finally, I said, "Okay, Barry, but if you see anybody, you let go of Pepper and run home screaming for me to come help you."

Barry and Pepper flew out of the gate. It was not five minutes when the neighbors came and told us that Barry and Pepper had found our things. Sure enough, about half way down the donga behind our house, Pepper stopped and started digging. The robbers had buried our things under a lot of brush. Pepper wanted to go on. But we picked up our things and headed back home. We gave Pepper a big steak for being such a good dog.

The next day the local police came to visit us. They had heard what our dog did and wanted to use her to help track some thieves. Barry brought Pepper around and she tried to attack the policemen. Wisely, they decided not to use Pepper. We knew we would not have any more problems with burglars; not in Morija, anyway. However, some very dear friends of ours were not so lucky.

While Joan and Jimmy were sitting in their back room reading, early one evening, they heard a loud noise, like glass breaking, coming from the front of the house. When Jimmy went out to the living room, he saw three masked men breaking into the front window of their home. Not knowing what to do, he grabbed a wooden statue and struck one man as he tried to enter. Then Jimmy ran and grabbed Joan. They barricaded themselves into the bedroom. They locked the door and pushed furniture in front of it, hoping to buy time until the police arrived.

Joan phoned the police and informed them that someone was breaking in. Within minutes, the thieves broke through the door and pushed the furniture back enough to enter the room. They grabbed Joan and stabbed her. Suddenly the phone rang. They yanked the phone wire out of the wall as Joan fell to the floor.

They kept shouting to Jimmy; "Give us all your money!"

There was no money in the house to give. They began to slash at Jimmy as he fought them. But the odds were against him and he fought until he collapsed. The thieves ran away, assuring Jimmy that they would return.

Jimmy was bleeding profusely, but his wounds were all superficial. Joan, on the other hand, was in more serious condition. Jimmy, seeing that she was still alive, dragged her outside to his little Volkswagen Beetle and drove her to the hospital.

At the hospital, the doctors were able to stop Joan's bleeding. She was injured seriously, but the attending physician assured Jimmy that she would live.

After treatment for his wounds, Jimmy left the hospital and went straight to the police station to try and find out why they did not respond to his call.

He approached the front desk. "Excuse me, I called to say that I had intruders in my house, and no one came. Do you know what happened?"

The man at the front desk directed Jimmy back to a ranking officer.

Needless to say, Jimmy was a little tense. He spoke to the officer in charge, "Sir, why did no one respond to my call for help?"

The officer looked up at him and said, "We called you back. You did not answer. We thought everything was okay."

Jimmy exploded, "Look at me! My wife was nearly killed by these hooligans and you don't even want to take the trouble to check my house? What kind of a police force is this?"

With that he stormed out of the police station.

It was a long, slow recovery for them. We spent many afternoons visiting Joan and Jimmy in their home. It took several months for her to get back to normal.

The physical injuries eventually healed, but there was no doctor who could take away the emotional scars that stayed after the break-in. Only through much prayer and dependence on the Lord were they able to overcome their fears.

They both continued their jobs teaching at Roma. Sometimes there were events to which they would go to at Roma on the weekends. It was a brisk cool afternoon in the middle of July of 1984 after one of these events that they were driving back from Roma in their Volkswagen Beetle. It was nearing dusk and they were eager to get back home. As they drove along, another car approached them from the opposite direction. Suddenly, the other car swerved into their lane and headed straight for them. They swerved off of the road to try to avoid the other vehicle, but it hit them head-on. They were both killed.

The driver of the other vehicle was unhurt. He had been drunk at the time of the accident.

Jimmy and Joan were buried in the Catholic cemetery at Roma on a sunny, windy afternoon. At the funeral we found comfort in the knowledge that these wonderful Christian people were in the arms of the Lord. But we knew that we would always miss them. It seemed that they were always there for us when we needed them. We would always remember them so fondly.

Times had not been easy, but we never had to face anything alone. I knew I was not alone now.

Chapter 30

ZOË GROWS

B arry tried to stay light-hearted. He told me how happy it made him that we had helped him settle into his new home. But, he couldn't hide his anxiety about our return to Africa.

"Mom, are you certain about this?"

"Yes, Barry, we can't leave your father alone over there any longer."

We all prayed for Charles' safety. As I earnestly prayed, I knew that many others whom we didn't even know about were praying as well. Our African church members gave so much into our lives and that really blessed us!

We stayed at Zoë Bible Church for several more years. During that time we were perpetually blessed by the Lord with strong growth in the church. More and more people became part of our fellowship through home cells and the feeding of the Word that went into our ministry. Pastor Dickson was filled with the Holy Spirit and developed into a mighty man of God and a loving leader. We even started a Christian school in the church.

The support of Hatfield Christian Church in Pretoria proved to be invaluable to us, especially in the early years. Because of them, we were able to attend most of the pastors' conferences in South Africa, usually in Johannesburg or Pretoria.

Often when we went to these meetings we would take our Hi-Ace filled with pastors from Lesotho. During one trip to Pretoria, Charles was not with me. I was driving our Hi-Ace with eight pastors from Lesotho. As we traveled, the South African police pulled the car over. They frequently checked for taxi licenses and made sure that the Kombie was not overloaded.

The policeman who stopped me looked into our vehicle and gasped.

"Madam, I need to see your taxi driver's license," he said.

I looked straight at him and explained, "This is not a taxi. I am a pastor's wife and I am taking all of these pastors to Pretoria."

Incredulously he asked, "You are doing this of your own free will?"

All of the pastors sat in stone silence, dreading what could possibly happen if there were a misunderstanding.

"Sir, we are serving in Lesotho. My husband and I have been working with these men as pastors in our church."

The policeman and his partner looked us over very carefully for what seemed to be an eternity.

The second one asked sternly, "You're sure that you are doing this voluntarily?"

"I assure you, officer, that no one has coerced me to do this. This is my car and this is what we do. These men are all honorable pastors and would never do any harm to me."

"All right, go ahead then, but watch who you trust."

"Thank you, officer."

We chuckled a bit recalling the look of total disbelief on the officers' faces as we gave thanks to God and rejoiced in His watch and care over us. We all had a wonderful trip to Pretoria and back.

We always held Sunday School in the local hospital, meeting in the children's wing. We usually started with praise and worship (the children loved the guitar) after which we would share a Bible story. Usually, we would try to have an illustration of some kind to help keep their attention.

One Sunday we were sharing the story of Adam and Eve in the garden of Eden and how the serpent tempted them. I had decided to bring a little red plastic snake to illustrate the serpent. The children listened eagerly as I began to relate the story of how the serpent tempted Eve. When I pulled the snake out of my bag, several of the children began to scream, terrified at the little plastic snake. Anyone who was mobile ran out of the room. Those who were bedfast hid their faces in their pillows. Within seconds I realized how terrified they were of snakes, even plastic ones.

After hiding the snake and apologizing to the children, we managed to get everyone back into the room. It was laughable, but not to them, so I held myself in check.

In spite of the snake blunder, at the end of the service we invited everyone to turn their hearts over to Jesus and accept Him as their Lord and Savior. At least five accepted Jesus as their Savior that day. I never, ever used even a picture of a snake again.

One lady, who truly desired to come to church, would get a violent headache every Sunday morning. Her relatives kept telling us that she was eager to come, but she could not walk the few blocks to the church. She was being treated for high blood pressure, so we decided to go and pray for her.

When we arrived at her hut, we found her in bed. We greeted her and then asked her to sit in a chair so that the four of us, Pastor Dickson, Me' Mathabo, Charles, and I could pray for her. She came to the middle of the room and sat in the chair, where we gathered around her. We anointed her with oil according to James 5:14 and prayed for her healing. As we prayed for her, she slumped down and her body slipped to the floor. She did not seem to be breathing! I could not find a pulse! My heart was racing trying to decide what to do.

As we were busy checking her, Pastor Dickson said, "Wait a minute! The devil is a liar! Let's just praise God and rejoice. We know God hears and He has already answered our prayers. Isaiah 65:24 says 'And it shall come to pass that before they call I will answer and while they are yet speaking, I will hear.' We will not be distracted by what we think we see; let's rejoice in the goodness of God and praise him for her healing!"

I stood along with everyone else and began to walk around the chair and her body lying on the floor. As we began to rejoice and praise the Lord, I momentarily forgot about the body on the floor and I could tangibly feel the presence of God in the room. Gradually my eyes fell to the chair and the floor. I was shocked to notice that there was no body on the floor. I quickly looked toward the bed and around the room, only to see the woman walking with us, with her hands lifted, praising God for her total healing. We all praised God for her healing and she never missed another church service. I especially praised God for Pastor Dickson's awesome faith.

One Saturday morning we went to Lancer's Gap to preach the good news of the Gospel to the people in the village up there. It was a beautiful day in the mountains and we expected many to come and hear the good news of Jesus.

We arrived at the village unannounced and went immediately to obtain permission from the chief to hold our services. At about noon we began to preach. By the time we finished, about fifteen people made a profession of faith. We began to pray for the sick people in the village. Many were healed instantly right there on the mountain in the warm sunshine.

Among those sick who asked for healing was a man who brought his son. He had a cough and a fever. He was healed immediately.

We continued to pray over the sick until almost 4:00 in the afternoon. Just as we were ready to leave, we were summoned to the chief's house. We wondered why we needed to see him again and then we thought, 'maybe he wants us to come back.' We were right.

When we arrived at his house we remembered him as the man who had brought his son to be prayed for. He was so grateful that he insisted we eat at his home. We were tired and hungry from the long day, so it was a welcome invitation. We also knew that we must not insult him by refusing his invitation.

After washing our hands in a pail of water outside, we entered his home. There we saw a table with a lovely cloth, and a tin bowl for each of us. As was the custom of the land, they did not join us, but only came in to serve us. We were treated to a dinner of beans, mealy pap, and chicken, along with something else which none of us were quite sure of. Since it would have been an insult not to eat everything that was served to us, we prayed over it and ate it all. We were so glad we had an opportunity to wash our hands because we had to eat our meal with our fingers. The family insisted that we eat all that we wanted before any of them ate. They seemed so happy to be able to share with us and serve us. This was not a prosperous area, so we did not take the seconds that they offered us, although it was tempting. We wanted to be sure that there was enough left for them. It was a blessed time for all of us, and we were grateful to God for his faithfulness.

In Morija, we had a Wednesday night prayer service in our home with about eighteen to twenty-four people. We would always begin with praise and worship, then we would pray in the power of the Holy Spirit, then in English, and then in Sesotho, being very specific about our requests. Because of these services we became very close to those who joined us.

One evening as we were praying, Tina came to me and urgently tapped me on the leg. When I looked up, she was frantically pointing toward the floor. There in front of us was a huge scorpion slowly walking our way. I quickly arose and walked past it into the kitchen to get a jar. The scorpion was so big that I was barely able to get the quart jar over it. I then slowly pulled the jar into the kitchen and left it in the corner with the scorpion under it.

The creature had probably walked in under our door or had come in on one of the blankets the people wore for protection against the cold night air. We were fortunate that no one was stung. The scorpion lived under that jar in the corner of our kitchen for over six weeks before dying.

We had a friend from church named Anna. During Easter of 1986 she wanted to visit her family in Bloemfontein. She told us the following story:

"I crossed the border into South Africa at about three in the afternoon. There was a young girl at the border with a baby who needed a ride to Bloemfontein so I gave her a ride. We had driven no more than thirty kilometers when I noticed a car approaching from behind at a very fast pace, so I pulled off of the shoulder to let him pass. The car passed and pulled right in front of my car, blocking me, and skidded to a stop. A very big man, a white South African got out of his car and started toward me. I've never seen such a man. He was huge! He wore shorts and a T-shirt, and no shoes. He had enormous feet. He was walking toward me fast with his fists clenched and his jaw set. He looked like he had fire spitting from his eyes. I remember thinking to myself, 'Is this man Satan?'"

"He yanked my car door open. I tried to smile and I said, 'What is the problem?'

"I was totally confused and bewildered by his apparent distress and anger."

"He started yelling at me and cursing and beating me with his fists, his eyes wild and furious looking. He just kept beating me. The young girl and baby beside me were trembling with fear. I was so shocked by the whole thing! He spoke in Afrikaans, which I cannot speak, but which I do understand very well. He kept shouting and cursing as he continued to beat me. Then he began kicking me in the side and in the hip area. I prayed, 'Dear Lord, forgive this man, for he knows not what he is doing.'"

"He then slammed my door shut so hard that the window jumped from its track and fell down into the door. He proceeded to kick the car, doing extensive damage to the door and the fender. He then stomped off in a huff, got into his own car and drove away in a fury of speed."

"I thanked the Lord for protecting me from this man, and then proceeded on my journey. I prayed for that man. Yes, I had met Satan face-to-face. It was truly horrible. My one arm was badly injured and swelling fast. I lifted my hand to Jesus and thanked Him for bearing my burdens on the cross. I laid my hand on my arm and thanked Jesus that He bore my iniquities and sickness. I thanked Him for healing my arm. Instantly the pain was gone. The swelling went down and I have had no discomfort from my injuries. Thank you, Jesus!"

Upon her return to Lesotho, Anna related the story to us. As she spoke of the man beating her, she quietly and slowly removed her sweater. I saw her arm. I could see the bruises. She had been badly beaten. I wanted to cry out for this injustice. One of my best friends had been badly mutilated, and what for? I felt an anger sweep over me such as I had never felt before. Anna was totally surprised at my reaction.

She said, "Come, Betty. Do not be angry. Let us praise the Lord together. Let us pray for the man, for I did not encounter the man, but Satan himself. I laughed at the devil for the rest of my journey."

So we praised God, and we prayed for the man, and we thanked God for protecting Anna.

There are so many other stories from those years at Zoë Bible Church. God was so faithful to us in manifesting His presence in the work of His church. It continues to grow still today in love, in faith and in numbers.

Gradually, we began to realize that if this church was to reach its full potential, we must leave. It was a Sesotho speaking church, and we were foreigners. Even though we were the outsiders, the people would always look to us for leadership and guidance. We knew that when we left, Pastor Dickson would take the reigns of leadership and he would grow stronger and bigger in Jesus. It was not an easy decision for us to make, but we knew that we must.

We met with Pastor Dickson and told him of our decision. He was disappointed, but he also knew that it was right. We agreed to be on an advisory board, but we would no longer attend this church. It was time for the people to see him as their pastor and spiritual leader.

As I thought of Pastor Dickson, I wondered what effects this war was having on him. Were he and his family safe? Was their church building destroyed? Had the church school been burned? I continued to pray and intercede for Charles and our friends.

Chapter 31

OBEDIANCE

The more I prayed, the more confident I felt about my escape. I knew exactly what I needed to do. First, I would take the license plates off my car. It would not be good for anyone to see plates from South Africa at this time.

My faith and courage began to build in preparation as well. I must keep praying about the right time to put my plan into action. As I continued in this way, I remembered another crossroads in our lives.

The time had come for us to leave Zoë, but what were we to do now? We knew that our time and ministry in Africa was not yet finished.

I had heard about a new church in Ladybrand, South Africa. I told Betty that I felt that we needed to look into it. Her immediate reaction was not good. In fact, she reminded me of our first trip to Ladybrand to purchase a car for M.C.C..

I remembered well how we were stared at, and considered how we would be accepted there. Ladybrand was a small town. Was it too small for my family? I wondered. But my feelings grew stronger and stronger that we must go to that church there.

I mentioned it to Betty again. She suggested that since I felt so strongly about it that I should go by myself and check it out. I knew she didn't really mean that. I also knew that was not what God was leading me to do. I kept praying about it.

The following Sunday, Betty, the kids and I crossed the border into Ladybrand to attend this new work. It was a small congregation of about twenty people, all white, except for an Indian couple and their children. They were meeting in a hall across from the police station. We slipped into the back of the church and took a seat.

Everyone seemed friendly. The pastor was obviously very warm and very spirit-filled. Immediately after praise and worship he said to the congregation, "Before you sit down, turn around and give somebody a hug,"

When the couple in front of us turned around, their mouths dropped open. We quickly extended our hands and introduced ourselves before we sat down. A hug would probably have been too much for them on this first Sunday.

As we attended this church over the next few weeks, Betty and I both began to realize that God was calling us to serve in this ministry. The third week we were there, the pastor invited us to have lunch with him.

Pastor At was a young pastor who had been raised in a church in Bloemfontein. God led him to Ladybrand to start this new church. He and his wife, Nyretta, started the church from scratch, with some support from his home church in Bloemfontein. They rented a small hall and started holding services. By the time we arrived, there were about twenty people who attended regularly. Ladybrand was a small town of about 3,000 people, but there were farms surrounding the community and a location near by, (where the black Africans are required to live) so there was great opportunity for growth.

Being invited to the pastor's house for lunch was quite a treat. Nyretta made a wonderful meal, after which we retired to the living room.

The conversation started with small talk, but gradually became more serious. It became apparent to us that the Pastor had done his homework. He spoke knowledgeably about some of our ministries, and knew much of the work we had previously done. Finally he asked, "What brought you to our church here in Ladybrand?"

I began to explain, "We are leaving our church in Maseru because we just think it's time for them to become more independent of us. They have a wonderful pastor who is a Mosotho, but they continually look to us for leadership. In order for them to grow, we had to leave."

"But as for why we came here," I continued, "I just felt the Spirit of God leading me here."

Pastor At smiled at my answer.

He continued, "You know, I dream of having a church where people of all races can worship and fellowship together. I think that God sent you here to help in this work."

What a radical idea this was! I could see clearly that God had given this anointed man of God a big vision. I knew in an instant that this was definitely where God was calling us. I wondered how God would orchestrate all of this. And, I reminded the pastor, "Do you recall that first Sunday we were in your service? You asked that we turn around and hug someone. The couple in front of us was so shocked to see us. Although we quickly shook their hands and introduced ourselves, we have not seen them in church since then. You could lose members when some of them see us in your church. Have you thought about that?"

He was adamant. "If we lose some, we will lose them, but in the long run the church has much more potential to grow as a mixed race church. I know God has called me to lead a church where people of all races can worship and fellowship together."

He continued, "I would really like for you to be a part of this church. You could do so much to help bridge the gap. Would you be willing to serve as a deacon, Charles?"

I had already spent much time in prayer about coming to Ladybrand. This was just the final confirmation, so I readily agreed to serve in any way.

During the next year we began to witness a steady growth in the church. Once they came to know us, people began to accept us pretty easily. Christian Revival Church was one of the first multi-racial churches in South Africa during these years of apartheid.

At this time, black South Africans were not considered to be citizens of the South African nation. They lived on homelands (locations), which made up about 14% of the land in South Africa. That meant that 80% of the population lived on 14% of the land. The remainder of the land, including the cities and the major mineral rich areas, were reserved for the whites. The poorest, most eroded land was left for the black population. Many of the black men moved into the South African locations to work in the mines and in the city industries. Their movement was strictly regulated and they had to remain segregated from the white population. Blacks were neither allowed to vote, nor to own land. They were therefore seen as transients, even though they may have lived in an area for several generations.

Not allowed to live in the urban areas, they settled in townships on the outskirts of cities. Ladybrand, as small as it was, had its own township a couple of kilometers away. They simply called it the "location." Soon after we started to serve in this church we began to reach out to the people in the location. Pastor At asked Pastor Edward (a black African) to come and assist him in building this work. He was a real asset to the ministry, reaching out to more people in the location.

At first it was difficult, but Pastor At continued to make the effort. On Sunday mornings, people would just naturally sit with other people whom they knew. As a result, when church started the black people would settle on one side and the whites on the other. Pastor At would get up and ask everyone to sit someplace else so that people would get to know each other and to fellowship in that way. The church continued to grow.

We continued to serve in any way that we could. Frequently, we would go to Sunday morning services, then go back to Morija for lunch (a good hours drive each way) and then return for Sunday evening services. Pastor At spoke to the congregation and asked if they would invite us for Sunday dinner to keep us from having to drive back home on Sundays. We were surprised at how many people were eager to do this. From then on, we enjoyed invitations to lunch by the white South African families every Sunday. With pleasure, we spent our Sundays getting to know different families better. One family in particular was especially kind to us and we even took naps in their home before the evening service.

Toward the end of our first year in Ladybrand, Pastor At came to see us. "Charles, what is God saying to you?"

I must admit, I was not exactly sure what he meant.

Pastor At continued, "Do you see change coming? Should you still be at the garage in Morija?

There was a moment of silence. Then I said, "I've really been praying about it."

"Continue to seek God and let's talk again next week." We then took a moment to pray for God's direction in our lives and His will in this ministry.

That night after church as we drove home, we talked about it.

Betty asked me, "Did you know this was coming?"

I told her that I hadn't anticipated this.

Betty continued, "What do you feel God wants us to do?"

One thing I was sure of, "I know this is of God."

Betty remained wary, "There will be a lot to do. Do you think we'll be able to find a place to live in that little town? Do you think anyone will rent to us?"

"You know, Betty, whenever we needed anything, God has always provided more than we expected. If this is His plan for us, He'll work out the details."

Experience had taught me well. As we pulled into our driveway in Morija, I knew that our time in this place would be short. That thought filled me with confidence and again, I knew this was of God. I looked forward to our 'new assignment' and I felt His peace, which gave me great comfort and assurance.

God had brought us through so many valleys and challenges. With His help, every change we went through was different but not too difficult and we ended up on a mountaintop.

This situation facing me right now looked much bigger than anything we went through in the past. But it surely didn't look so very big to God. I continued to pray and to prepare for my escape.

Chapter 32

SOUTH AFRICA

I jumped when the phone rang. I was hoping it was Charles. "Hello?"

Charles' older brother, Jim, and his wife, Janet, answered. Unlike other friends and family members who had called, they were very encouraging and stood with me, strong in faith. They prayed with me and heartened me with assurances that God was with us both and He is always more than enough.

I was blessed by their call. They had often been a source of strength to us. Both Charles and I had felt the power of their prayer covering.

I remembered how much we needed that strong covering when we moved from Lesotho to South Africa.

There was so much to do. First, Charles had to give notice to the Lesotho Evangelical Church that he would give up management of the garage. That was a bittersweet moment for Charles. On one hand he looked forward with great anticipation to the new ministry God was opening up for him.

On the other hand, he had worked very diligently to make the garage a growing concern. It was now making a profit, which it had never done before. Charles' success had even allowed him to make some structural improvements to the garage; a new office and a new parts room. Now it was time to move on. Charles wasn't sure who to leave in charge. The transition would take at least six to eight weeks to complete.

Another concern we faced was finding housing in Ladybrand. Apartheid was still the law in most areas of South Africa. I had more than a little trepidation about being accepted into a community of Afrikaners, and what the many problems could be. Of course, by this time we were very much accepted by members of our congregation, but not everyone in Ladybrand belonged to our congregation.

In addition, we had heard about bands of marauding black Africans who would go to farms to rob and murder families, trying to drive them from the land. Unfortunately, Ladybrand was a particularly opportune place for these crimes. Some of the farms overlooked the Caledon River, which was the border to Lesotho. A small group could easily cross this river illegally, create havoc on a farm and slip quietly back into Lesotho where they could blend into the population without fear of detection or retribution.

The news constantly reported on these murders taking place. All of our friends advised us against living outside of town, but the house that became available to us was in the countryside. Pastor At heard about a farm not too far from church. The farmer had rented his land to other farmers and the house was sitting empty.

The house was big and roomy with a nice big coal cooking stove in the kitchen and another nice stove in the family room. The carpeted sunroom remained furnished with the farmer's furniture and looked extremely pleasant. The front part of the house had a small, self-contained area consisting of a sitting room, a bedroom and a bathroom. It functioned as a small apartment separate from the rest of the house. And, the rent was very reasonable.

After walking through it, we decided to take it despite warnings from our friends. At the time I was more afraid of the reprisals from the Afrikaners around us than I was of any attacks from across the border.

In Morija, our furniture had been provided with the house. We needed lots of furniture for this house. Pastor At spoke to the congregation one Sunday and mentioned our needs. Different families in Ladybrand donated furniture and even delivered it to our new home. We were really blessed by their continual acts of love.

Barry decided to claim the little apartment for himself. He really enjoyed the privacy. By this time he had finished high school and was working for a living.

Living in the farmhouse became truly a blessing for Tina. Our neighbors on the next farm were members of the church and they raised Appaloosa horses. Tina and I had our own horses and often rode over to their farm. When Clair saw that Tina was such a good rider she asked her to help train her horses for the annual endurance race. Tina rode almost every day and really loved it.

Near sunset one evening, there was a knock at our door. When I went to the door there stood soldiers from the South African army. My heart nearly stopped! After all, our marriage went against the laws of the land.

But, they weren't there to arrest us. They had come to help us. The army had received intelligence that there were to be attacks on farms in the area. The soldiers introduced themselves and issued us a weapon along with a radio so that we could stay in contact with the other farmers around us. They also took time to instruct us on how to use the weapon. It was a very hi-tech rifle equipped with a night-vision scope. I was amazed to discover how far I could see into the darkness using that scope. After using it a few times to look into the night, we leaned it up against the wall, and that's where it stayed. Since we still didn't know the neighbors, except for Clair and Bernard, we never hooked up the radio.

Thank God, the attackers never came to our house. Almost every night we heard shots, but afterwards heard very little about the cause. The one thing we did know was that the blood of Jesus Christ is more than enough and our God was big enough to keep us in His tender care. We knew that we had nothing to fear.

Little by little, our neighbors came to introduce themselves. I found that my misgivings about living among the Afrikaners were greatly misplaced. All of our neighbors treated us wonderfully.

Tina continued to train for the race with Clair. We became close friends with Clair and Bernard and their family. They visited us or we visited them almost every week for a meal and fellowship together. After months of training together, Clair insisted that Tina had enough skill and talent to enter the South African endurance race. This was a long horse race fairly unique to South Africa. The horses and their riders would run for three days for about 80 kilometers per day in all kinds of terrain. Some of the trails were so rugged that the riders could only walk their horses through them.

When Tina applied to enter, she was accepted immediately. After the application was accepted, Clair mentioned that Tina was not white. This created a real problem for the race officials. Clair fought them to allow Tina to compete. Finally, the officials relented on the condition that Tina was not really an African. She had entered the race and the country on a Canadian visa. Apartheid had reared its ugly head once again.

In preparation for the race, Clair cautioned Tina that since this was her first race she probably would not win anything. No one had ever placed their first time out or, for that matter, no first timer had ever even finished the race. Claair simply hoped that Tina would make a good showing and do her best. However, Tina did not accept that limited vision. She was going to ride to win.

Tina and I went to the little town that hosted this event. All the horses were in the local park. We slept in our Kombi in the park and cooked our meals on an open fire. Some of the riders stayed in tents. People were selling hot dogs and there was always soda and cold water to drink. Tina and Clair rode their horses and I waited (along with many others) at the rest stops to rub down the horses with rags soaked in cool water. The vets checked the horses at each rest stop. That first night Tina was so tired she refused food and went straight to bed. The second night she was in so much pain she could not get comfortable. I rubbed her back and her legs until she finally fell asleep. I became concerned that this type of race was too hard on the horses and on the riders; but Tina remained determined to continue.

As we waited at the finish line, we expected the unexpected. Knowing Tina and her strong ambition to achieve whatever she set her mind to, we knew that this race would be no exception. We watched with excited anticipation. When Tina crossed the finish line, she was in third place; something that had never been done in that competition by a first-timer. Proudly, she received her medal. The crowd was stunned that she was not white; and she not only placed, she placed third.

We all attended a banquet that night where the medals were given out. Only Afrikaans was spoken, so we understood nothing of what was said until they called Tina's name. Even recognizing her name was difficult because the pronunciation was so different. Others had to tell us when the announcer called her up to receive her medal. How amazing it was to see God using us to pull down strongholds in South Africa, even in an endurance race.

We worked for two years at Christian Revival Church in Ladybrand as assistant pastors, nurturing and helping it grow. During that time, the Lord led Pastor At into a building program and we were able to complete a new thatched roof church, debt-free. We served the people at this church with great joy and enthusiasm and looked forward with delight to our work every day.

Pastor George Goodyear from Bloemfontein was Pastor At's close friend and mentor for many years. When the phone call came that Pastor George had suffered a massive heart attack and was now in the presence of Jesus Christ, it caught us all by surprise. And, we all felt devastated. We knew that Pastor George was in heaven, but his absence left a big gap, in fact, in our lives and in the ministry. This event set us into a time of great prayer and seeking God. We knew major changes would be coming our way.

Not long after the funeral, Pastor At sat down and told us that God was calling him back to Bloemfontein to pastor that church. Although, we had been expecting it, we did not want to face it. Pastor At asked us to move into the position of the senior pastors in Ladybrand. We definitely did not feel ready for this awesome responsibility. Helping Pastor At and serving him was one thing, but for us to become the senior pastors we wondered how this was even possible. Apartheid was still in full force and this was a little town in South Africa. Would the people still look at us as leaders? However, we knew God is big enough and if this was God's plan it would work. After much prayer we believed this was God's plan and we would see God's power as we continued to serve Him and obey Him.

On the Sunday before he left, Pastor At preached a powerful, encouraging sermon. At the close of the service, he brought us up to the front of the church and said to the congregation, "These are your pastors just as I am your pastor. You need to accept them, love them, and respect them just as you have accepted, loved and respected me." Everyone came forward to give us a big hug and encourage us in our new position as their leaders.

What a miraculous thing God had done! He had taken us, two people who had fled racial persecution in America, and planted us in a small Afrikaans community living under Apartheid. Our congregation, both black and white, readily accepted us as their pastors. What a mighty God we serve! He was changing hearts and changing history. When we attended the annual pastors' meetings at Rhema in Johannesburg, people often asked us who the new pastor was in Ladybrand. It always amused us to see the surprised look on their faces when we told them that we were the pastors there.

One Sunday morning after Charles had finished his sermon and dismissed the congregation, a man rushed up to the front of the church so fast that our deacons stopped him before he could get to Charles.

In their grasp, he shouted to Charles in a demanding voice, "Who are you?"

Charles politely introduced himself.

"No! No!" he said. "I want to know, WHO ARE YOU?"

For a few minutes, Charles tried to figure out what he meant.

After a couple of minutes, the man calmed down and said, "This is my first time to visit your church. I was so surprised to see so many 'different' people all here together. Your sermon was so good. I want to know who you are and where you are from."

Finally Charles realized what he meant. This white man just did not understand how it was possible for him to hear an intelligent message from a black man. Charles would give no answer. He was just a man trying to be obedient to God's call. The power and the glory all go to God.

Without a doubt, I know that God's angels surround us; now and always.

Chapter 33

THE CROSS

As I walked outdoors to scout and plot out my escape, I could barely see. The sounds of fighting continued around me, and the smell of acrid smoke was stinging my throat. I spoke out loud Psalm 46, verse 1, "God is my refuge and strength, a very present help in trouble." And, verse 10: "Be still and know that I am God."

Although my circumstances had not appeared to change, I felt reassured and comforted. In my impending journey, I knew that He was the only one who could help me now; through both the expected and the unexpected. I was trying not to be too surprised by the unexpected, which I had faced on many different occasions.

In 1985, while in Chester visiting our families, we decided to go to Wal Mart to pick up a few things. The sun shone brightly as we drove out to the store. Betty went over the shopping list as I drove. The parking lot was not too crowded since it was the middle of the week. As we took a shopping cart, we noticed a couple of elderly ladies ahead of us, about thirty feet away. After a closer look, I noticed that one was Miss Fondren, a teacher from high school who had given me so much difficulty when the schools were first integrated. It had been over forty years since that had taken place, and I found myself wondering if she would be pleased to see me. Betty caught my eye and I saw that she too had seen Miss Fondren.

My mind flashed back to an unpleasant moment in Miss Fondren's classroom when I was a freshman in high school and I was totally unprepared by my elementary (negro school) education.

"Charles," she asked, "can you tell me what predicate nominative is in this sentence?"

I had no idea what she was talking about, so I said nothing.

"Do you know the answer?" she queried.

I slowly shook my head to indicate that I did not know.

She then turned to the rest of the class saying with mock sweetness, "This is why these students should not be in school here."

Just as I snapped out of memory lane, Miss Fondren turned around and noticed us. She looked intently for just a second and then started walking toward us.

"Charles McGee. Charles McGee," she repeated.

After all these years, she looked much as she had when I was in school. Relieved, I saw that she had a big smile on her face. As I looked into her eyes, I noticed tears welling up.

"Charles McGee," she said as she took my hand gingerly and kept holding it.

At this point, we could both see tears streaming down her face. For a moment she just stood there holding my hand, unable to speak.

Finally she said, "Charles, I treated you very badly when you were my student. I was so wrong, and I'm so sorry."

We waited, not sure what to say.

She continued, "I was so wrong. Please forgive me."

Without hesitation I replied, "It's okay, Miss Fondren, I forgave you long ago."

She stood there for the longest time with tears streaming down her face.

Finally I said, "The past is forgiven and forgotten. Don't give it another thought."

She collected herself and began to chat. "I hear you've been serving God in Africa."

We took a few minutes to share a little with her about our work in Africa. She seemed genuinely pleased, even proud. She said, "We'll be praying for you and your family."

With that we both parted and did the rest of our shopping. On the way home Betty commented, "She had been waiting years to do that."

"Yes she had," I replied. "I'm really glad that we met her like we did. I'm sure that's a load off of her mind."

"That wasn't an accident was it?" Betty asked.

"I don't believe that there are accidents. God has a plan for each and every detail of our lives," I responded.

Betty touched my hand as we rode home in silence, overjoyed at the healing power of God.

However, not all of our visits brought reconciliation and refreshment. During another home leave in the 90's, we went to visit Betty's mother who had moved to a very small town in southern Missouri. It was a wide spot in the curve of the tarmac road consisting of ten to fifteen houses, a barber shop, a post office, and a tavern. Everyone knew everyone, and it seemed to be a pleasant little place.

We arrived on a particularly hot and sultry day on Friday evening. Most of the people in town were on their front porches enjoying the soft breeze before the sunset and before the onset of mosquitoes that would come out immediately after the sun went down.

As we came around the curve in the road, we spotted the house and pulled into the driveway. It felt good to get out of the car and stretch our legs.

As we piled out of the car, we heard a neighbor call out to Betty's Mom, "Hazel, are these your kids coming in?"

"Yes!" Mom shouted back to her. "They're finally here."

After some hugs and kisses, we all went into the house for dinner. It was good to be together again.

We spent our Saturday together doing a few things around the house, but mainly catching up on the past few years. On Sunday, of course, we went to church.

This was not our first visit at this small community church. We had been here before, so we knew most of the people. It was an all white church except when we came.

Betty's mom introduced us to their new pastor with great pride, telling him that we were missionaries from Africa. He behaved in a very warm and friendly manner toward us.

When the pastor opened his mouth to preach, he began to speak on the presence of sin in our lives and how dangerous it is to us. "Sin is like a big black cloud hanging over us. We must chase it from our lives. We even see on TV that the bad guy is usually dressed in black with a black hat and the good guy is usually dressed in white, oftentimes riding a white horse. If we want a close relationship with God, we must get rid of all the black in our lives. Remember, black is always bad and white is always good."

When those last words came out of his mouth, he looked right at us, and his face paled. In that moment, he realized that what he had said was not what he meant. Indeed, he really had said all the wrong things. He looked as if he hoped the ground would swallow him up. Unfortunately for him, he stood in front of his entire congregation.

Totally flustered, he looked at us and, trying to smile, said weakly, "Mr. McGee, I am not referring to you. I'm just using an illustration."

Both Betty and I smiled uncomfortably and nodded. Quickly, he went on to the next portion of scripture, but his sermon ended rather quickly and rather abruptly.

After the service as we greeted people and prepared to leave, the pastor approached us. He apologized profusely, once again, for the blunder during his message.

Finally he said, "Mr. McGee, I would be honored if you would bring the message tonight."

Since I felt he was just attempting to make amends, I smiled broadly, "That's okay. You don't need to do that."

"No, please. I would like for you to deliver the sermon in the evening service."

Since he seemed in earnest, I readily agreed.

That evening, I spoke on Ephesians six and using the armor of God against our enemy, the devil. Afterwards, the pastor came up to us again, thanking me for the wonderful sermon and saying, "You can preach in my church any time."

After the service ended, our friends invited us over for fresh strawberries and ice cream. What a treat!

When we got home to Betty's mother's house, it was 10:30 and I was thoroughly exhausted. The kids and I went straight to bed. Betty stayed up for one last cup of tea with her Mom.

At about half past eleven, I felt Betty climb into bed beside me. She fell asleep almost immediately. Now, I lay awake. The air felt still and very hot. We slept in the living room on a hide-a-bed couch and because of the heat we had left the front door open to let in some air, although the screen door was locked. Unable to fall back asleep, I began to pray and talk to God.

As I prayed, I heard a truck with a loud muffler outside. I thought it was probably visiting one of the neighbors. Suddenly, the room filled with a yellow glow and then I heard the truck speed away. My first thought was that God had come into the room as I prayed and worshipped Him. However, as I looked closer, I saw that the yellow glow was flickering. I heard a funny crackling sound, like that of a fire.

Curious, I quietly slid out of bed and walked cautiously to the front door to look out. What I saw made my heart pound with a combination of anger, fear, and unbelief. There right in front of me, just outside our front door, was a huge burning cross at least six feet tall. I stood and stared at it not knowing what to do.

How could this be? I thought that this type of thing had ended in America long ago. Civil rights had triumphed and the specter of racial hatred and discrimination had been vanquished, hadn't it? How could this be?

I numbly walked over to the bed, shook Betty and whispered, "Honey, I think you need to see this."

Stirring, she mumbled, "What is it?"

"Just look out the front door."

My heart continued to race as she snapped awake and sprang out of bed to look out the front door. We both just stared in unbelief.

I couldn't seem to tear my eyes away from that awful sight. Without turning away from it, I said to Betty, "Honey, you'd better wake your mom."

Awakened by the commotion, Barry walked in and looked outside. Without words for a minute, he finally turned his face to me and asked, "Dad, is this satanic, or is this racial?"

"Son, it's both."

Betty tried to gently wake her mother, but she awoke with a start. "What is it? Is it Ed?"

"No, Mom," Betty replied. "Ed's fine, but there is a burning cross right outside our front door."

Mom jumped up and shouted, "Oh my goodness. Where's my gun?"

"Mom, please, just phone the police. We don't need a gun."

In just a few minutes, the police arrived. Betty and I walked outside to meet them and tell them all that we knew.

As we looked around, we could see most of the neighbors on their front porches, watching the cross burn.

One policeman took me by the arm and ushered me into the house. "I think you need to stay in here for your own protection, sir."

Blessedly, Tina slept through the entire ordeal. When she awoke the next morning she was quite surprised to find police in the house asking questions.

During a more relaxed moment, one of the officers sat chatting with Tina and asked, "So, what's it like living in South Africa?"

Tina replied, "It's a beautiful country, the people are friendly, and they have never burned a cross in our front yard."

The police stayed with us, in our home for the rest of our visit with Betty's family. They insisted we not go outside for our own protection. We felt like we were under house arrest.

During another home visit, an unexpected blessing developed. A new evangelical church had formed in Chester. My brother, Walter, and his wife, Joyce, had joined as members of this new church. God richly blessed this work and it grew rapidly to be one of the largest congregations in Chester.

Joyce arranged for us to meet with the pastors of this new church. The pastors asked us to speak in the Sunday service. Of course we never turned down an opportunity like that at any church, especially when it involved family.

To our surprise, after that Sunday, we received some financial support from that church every month for the rest of our time overseas. What a blessing that was to our ministry! God continued to provide for us in every way as we faithfully served in Africa.

However, at this moment, I confessed, "Yes, Lord, I'm still glad we're in Africa; but I feel more than ever that I need to get out now. I want to collect Betty, Tina and Sharon at the airport. Lord, please help me!"

I picked up my Bible and began to read in the Psalms.

Chapter 34

Revival

As I began packing my bags for the flight back to Africa, I fought back tears. Why couldn't Charles have gotten out of there BEFORE all of this erupted? Was I indeed foolish to be flying back to a country in the midst of such political upheaval? And, thinking practically, would Charles even be out in time to meet us at the airport?

I refused to imagine that he could be hurt. I made my mind picture angels round about him with huge swords and big shields. And, I knew that God would provide transportation for us from the airport. I expected to see Charles waiting for us there.

I dried my eyes and thought about how we had escaped from many difficult situations.

I felt almost desolate and abandoned with the impending move of Pastor At from Ladybrand. Part of the reason for this was that I felt ill-equipped and unprepared to serve as one of the senior pastors at the church. The special friendship and trust that Charles and I had grown used to and depended upon would become a long distance relationship. I wanted so very badly to have some time away to really hear from God about all of this. It should have come as no surprise to find that God already had a special plan to heal my heart.

Pastor At invited me and Mrs. George Goodyear to Johannesburg to join him in attending a series of special meetings being held by Dr. Rodney Howard-Browne. By 6:00 a.m. in the morning we were on our way. We arrived just in time for the 10 a.m. meeting and were seated in the third row from the front. This particular meeting was not open to the public but was for pastors only. Dr. Browne had an excellent message, but we could not help but notice some strange things happening round about us. People all over the building began to laugh, some were even shaking horribly, while others groaned and made funny sounds. It actually appeared kind of comical from where we sat. Mrs. Goodyear and I began to giggle a bit ourselves at all the hilarity around us.

As the meeting drew to a close, Dr. Browne asked if there were any pastors present dealing with issues in their lives. He wanted all those pastors to come to the front and turn their issues over to God. He pointed out that God wanted us free, totally free, so that we could more easily minister to His people.

Pastor At encouraged me to go forward for prayer. I did not want to go, so I slipped out and went to the ladies room. I came out to find Pastor At close by, watching and waiting for me. Again, he insisted that I go up front for prayer. I reluctantly obeyed. Dr. Browne was speaking, "I want to come and lay hands on you and pray for each one of you." I thought, 'Lord, if all this that is happening is really from You, You touch me and You deal with me. I don't need this man to lay hands on me.'

After that, I'm not even sure how it happened, but the next thing I knew I was flat on the floor. I felt as if my back had been pinned to the ground. Then I had a weird sensation. It was as if huge claws started in the middle of my back and seemed to rip or tear right up my back and over my right shoulder. I actually felt pain. I screamed and tried to sit up.

At that instant, (and I knew, that I knew, it was God) I heard "I AM HERE! YOU HAVE NOTHING TO FEAR." I became aware that He had removed all my doubts, all my fears, all my anger and even all my questions. My heart was full to overflowing with His peace and His love. I began to cry tears of joy. It seemed like only minutes and my soft sobbing turned into laughter as it is written in Proverbs 17:22, "A merry heart doeth good like a medicine, but a broken spirit drieth the bones."

I laughed and I laughed and it felt so good. Again, it seemed like only minutes and then I lay very still. As I tried to open my eyes, they opened easily. I sat up, and there was Pastor At right beside me, helping me up. I smiled at him and looked around me. To my amazement, no one remained in the building but my friends who had been waiting for me. They told me that I had been on the ground for almost two hours. There, they saw me rolling, crying, and laughing.

Chapter 35

NEW LIFE

I was beginning to see that God wanted to touch all of His children in a special way to bring refreshing, healing and new life. Job 8, verse 21, "Till he fill thy mouth with laughing, and thy lips with rejoicing" was indeed true.

During the next year, we saw the Holy Spirit move in a mighty way. Our church membership grew to almost four hundred people. We were completely accepted and supported. Many times when Charles would begin to preach, people would laugh and fall to the floor. Under the leading of the Holy Spirit, we would give an altar call to accept Jesus and there would be many salvations–sometimes more than twenty people in one service. Often, we would call people to the front for healing and as we stepped towards them, they would fly back and hit the floor. Church services that used to last an hour or so were now two to three hours long. Many were saved and many were healed. The power of God became evident in all of our lives.

During this mighty move of God in Christian Revival Church in Ladybrand, we decided to hold Friday night prayer meetings from eight until midnight. We didn't even bother to put up chairs, because everyone was on the floor praying and seeking the face of God. People were given prophesies, a word of knowledge, a word of wisdom and many were simply being born again.

Some of the youth who attended our church in Ladybrand went to Machabeng High School in Maseru. Two of the young ladies decided to meet in a small room to pray during their lunch break at school. They prayed faithfully every day for the other students. Day by day, more and more students would join them in their prayers. Within two weeks, the room was packed with students on their knees praying. Many of the students in the school discovered how much Jesus loved them and were filled with the Holy Spirit, praying and praising God just as in the book of Acts, "And it shall come to pass in the last days, saith God, I will pour out of my Spirit upon all flesh and your sons and your daughters shall prophesy, and your young men shall see visions, and your old men shall dream dreams." The students preferred to pray rather than eat lunch or take part in other school activities.

One of our church elders lived in Maseru. He and his wife started having Friday night prayer meetings with this group of young people. Each week, more young people came. The group would pray and praise God in song together for hours. They were so hungry for more of God in their lives...and they were being filled.

Now that we were the senior pastors at the church with more responsibilities than ever before, we moved from the farm into town. We purchased a house not far from church on Botha Street. The house was more than 100 years old and located next to a nursing home. At one time, it had served as the first hospital in the area. Since it was considered a historic building, we were unable to make any changes on the outside. That didn't bother us, because it was beautiful. We bought it for a reasonable price and it turned out that the payments were less than rent would have been.

A young couple moved into the farmhouse. The husband worked at the American Embassy in Maseru and his wife was a lecturer at Roma University. We prayed that they would be as happy as we had been living there. However, a few months after they moved in, a group of renegades broke into their home in the early morning hours to rob them. They beat him badly and gang-raped her and her sister, who was visiting at the time, right in front of him. As horrible as it was, they were all very grateful to be alive. We visited them and prayed with them and saw God work to heal their lives. They boldly stayed on at the farm and saw no more acts of violence.

During this time, Barry decided to move back to the United States to continue his education. This was not easy for me, or for the ministry (because he was our sound man) but Charles and I knew that it was the best thing for him. Barry had been working in several different jobs; part-time as a chef and part-time in computers; but definitely had not been finding his full potential here in Africa. We spoke to Charles' brother Don, who lived in a Chicago suburb at the time. Don and his family were more than willing to take Barry in so that he could go to community college. We missed him terribly and although we had the bittersweet feelings of seeing our son leave us, we knew that it would truly be best for him.

The Christian Revival Church in Ladybrand continued its amazing growth. And in Bloemfontein, Pastor At's church grew exponentially. The Christian Revival Church expanded throughout the entire country of South Africa. Churches sprung up in Klerks Dorp, Cape Town, Kroon Stad, and Pretoria. A church also began in Botshabelo, a homeland between Ladybrand and Bloemfontein.

We would gather regularly with pastors from our affiliate churches to pray together and share our ideas. And, we always discussed areas in which to expand. One of the most obvious places was Maseru. In Maseru, there were hundreds of people from throughout Africa, as well as Europe and the Western Hemisphere. There were only two Evangelical churches in Maseru, and both were Sesotho-speaking churches. We felt there was a real need for an English-speaking church to be planted there. Each time we met, we prayed for a pastor or a couple to take on this challenge.

During this time, Tina married a blonde, blue eyed, white South African. She had a beautiful wedding with a reception in our garden. At that point, she was also granted permanent residence in South Africa. It seemed easy for her, so she encouraged us to do the same. Permanent residence would mean that we wouldn't have to renew our visa every three years, which took a substantial amount of time and money.

We applied for permanent residence, fully expecting that it would take a while but with confidence that it would eventually be approved. Finally, a letter came in the mail from the South African immigration service. When I opened it, I was horrified to see that not only had our application been denied, but we had only fifteen days to leave the country.

I thought, "How could this be? There must be some mistake."

After a few moments, I picked up the telephone and called Pastor At. Amazingly, I got right through to him.

"Pastor At?" I said.

"Hi, Betty, what's happened?"

"Well, I have some bad news."

"Oh?"

"We received a letter from immigration today."

I proceeded to read the entire letter to him.

After a slight pause, Pastor At exclaimed, "Praise the Lord! That's confirmation!"

"Confirmation?" I asked.

"You're the ones who are supposed to go to Maseru."

"Really?"

"Yes, we've known all along that you're the ones who are supposed to go to Maseru. Think about it! You lived there for years. You know your way around. You've had experience in church planting. You know the people. You know the customs. You're perfect for the church there."

"Okay," I said, but I was not convinced.

When Charles came home, we spent that night talking and praying about what to do. Finally we said, "Okay, we've got fifteen days to move. Lord, if this is of You, You're going to have to sell this house in fifteen days. Not only that, You're going to have to find us a place to live and a place to have church. There is no way we can do all of this on our own."

Charles, certain that this was a call from the Lord, never lost confidence. But I still felt shaken and unsure.

The next day we went over to Maseru and trudged through the streets looking for a building to hold church services and for a house in which to live. We did not find a single thing. Everywhere we went, doors seemed closed to us.

The next day, we arose early and spent an hour and a half in prayer before we left. As we drove to Maseru, Charles said, "The Lord is saying we must go to this school and inquire."

"If you say so." I replied. "We don't know anybody at that school anymore. I'm not even sure who to talk to."

Regardless, we went to the school to inquire. They immediately rented us the hall for the reasonable rate of R100 per hour. Most places had wanted R500-800 per hour. We signed the lease for a year, pleased that we found a place that would seat 150 people.

Houses in Maseru rent for about R6000 per month. That equates to about $900 per month, which was completely out of our budget. But we began to search, more optimistic than before, since the Lord had provided our church hall.

On that same day, I had been invited to a Bible study and had agreed to go. Why? I didn't know and I had so much to do. There is a time and a purpose for everything, but I didn't think that this was the time for a Bible study. Besides, I dreaded that it would end up like so many Bible studies where the conversation would deteriorate into a debate about some controversial subject. I didn't need that kind of thing right now. I had other, more important things to do, like finding a house! However, I had given my word that I would go, so grudgingly, I decided to honor that word.

Occasionally throughout the day before, I complained to Charles, "Why am I going to this Bible study? I know exactly what it's going to be."

He encouraged me and said "I know God has a perfect plan. It will be okay."

I was still reluctant to go to the Bible Study the next morning. Because of all the unrest in Lesotho, these meetings were never held at night. I just felt I had too much to do and perhaps I could spend my time more wisely..

Sure enough, the meeting went in the direction I had feared. A debate broke out about whether or not God hears and answers prayers. Of course, I knew from experience that God always hears and answers our prayers when we pray according to the Word of God.

One woman in particular was getting very upset until I finally took her by the hand and said, "You know, Jesus really loves you and cares for you, no matter what you may think."

She stared at me blankly for a moment, and then I saw her eyes grow moist with tears.

"Does he really?" she asked in a doubtful tone.

"Do you realize that if you had been the only person on earth Jesus Christ would still have died on the cross for you?"

"Well, I do, but…"

She ended up giving her life to the Lord right there. I knew then that was the reason I was supposed to be at that Bible study. I don't know who rejoiced over her more, me or the angels. I realized that this was much more important than finding a house to live in. Eventually, this same lady became a very faithful member of our church in Maseru and continued to grow in the power of the Lord. I was so sorry I had almost missed this opportunity God had provided for me.

We all prayed together before parting. Just as everyone was about to leave, our hostess called out to us, "Does anyone know anyone who would like to rent a house for R1,000 a month?"

In a flash, I jumped up, "I would!"

Upon learning more about the house, I agreed to rent it sight unseen. Later, when Charles and I walked through it, we found it to be perfect for our needs. And, even better, we could move in by the weekend.

Driving back to Ladybrand, our only remaining concern was to sell our home. The next morning we listed it with a realtor. That afternoon, the realtor brought a couple by to look at it. They decided to purchase it that day. Normally it takes about two months for the sale of a house to close, but somehow, ours closed in two weeks.

As every one of these details fell perfectly into place, we knew that the call back to Maseru was definitely of God. We were also praising God for the Afrikaans man and his wife who had been raised up to become the pastors in Ladybrand. At our final service in Ladybrand, we bade farewell to the congregation. Since the entire move was such short notice to us, it was more than short notice to the rest of the congregation. Our members expressed shock and disappointment to see us go.

As we said our final farewells to the people, one man stopped us for a conversation. He said to Charles, "You know, Charles, when I first saw you and your wife, honestly, I was so shocked. I could not tolerate it. But now I've grown to love you both so very much."

He then gave us both a big hug.

As people kept coming to us to say good bye and give us a hug, we marveled at the changes God had made in the lives of these people. One such person was a lady who had started attending church while we were on home leave. Often during the message the Pastor would mention that he was looking forward to our coming back. When we did get back, she was shocked and offended to see that we were a mixed couple. Immediately, she went to Pastor At to demand how he could allow this in his church. Our Pastor pointed out to her that Moses' wife was an Ethiopian. He continued on that being 'unequally yoked' was speaking of believers with unbelievers. On her own, she continued to search God's Word to find a basis to oppose our marriage on her own. Instead, the more time she spent in the Word, the more God began to speak to her and convict her about her objections to our marriage. Eventually, she made an appointment to come and see me. When she arrived, she burst into tears and begged me to forgive her. I hugged her and forgave her; we prayed together, and we became very good friends.

Another lady pointed out to Charles that it had been a shock to her and her husband to see us, a mixed couple. Slowly, but surely they grew to love us dearly. To emphasize her acceptance she said she wanted to kiss Charles right on the mouth. Having said that, she gave him a big hug and kissed him, right on the mouth!

Another lady felt that Charles seemed reluctant to hug her and she wanted a big hug from him every Sunday.

That day, we praised God for all these wonderful Afrikaans people. They so lovingly accepted us and taught us so much. The laws of Apartheid may go away with legislation, but the spirit of Apartheid will only go away with God's love.

The reality of God's love surrounded me and lifted me up right then and there. Although I ached for a phone call from Charles, to hear that he had escaped the killing and burning and turmoil in Maseru, I felt peace. God could handle anything.

Chapter 36

MASERU

W hat is that vibration? Then I saw it; a huge tank came rumbling down our street. Soldiers sat on top of it, scanning the landscape for trouble. They looked straight at our house. I quickly ducked out of view. Could this be the Lesotho Army? I don't think so! Maybe this is good news. Lord, I prayed, are they here to help me?

Uncertain of their intentions, I hid myself, abandoning my escape preparations for the moment. Suddenly my thoughts raced back to when we moved back to Maseru to start the church here.

It was March of 1997. The seed had already been planted by the students' prayer meetings. The lady whom Betty had met in the Bible study became a member right away. On Saturdays we were in the streets of Maseru, witnessing Jesus' love to all who would listen.

We began our church with a core of believers. Our ministry was based on the love of God, the truth of the Gospel and the leading of the Holy Spirit. The Lord brought a wonderful Ethiopian couple to us to be elders in the church. We met with them faithfully every week and they were of great assistance to us. We shared meals together, and always spent time praising and worshipping God. We loved them more and more and we also became very fond of their traditional foods.

The ministry grew steadily. We held leaders' meetings every Tuesday and taught on integrity and commitment. We held home cells on Wednesdays and they became very successful. The youth cell met on Saturdays. With all the growth, we began to see a need for proper sound equipment. Having a big vision for the church, we priced the equipment we felt we would need. It came to R27,000. After much prayer and thought, we decided to present this need to the church.

Sunday morning came and we preached on David and Goliath:

1 Sam 17:36 says, "Your servant killed both the lion and the bear; and this uncircumcised Philistine shall be as one of them, for he has defied the armies of the living God."

In verse 37, David said, "The Lord, who delivered me out of the paw of the lion and out of the paw of the bear, He will deliver me out of the hand of this Philistine..."

David knew God was on his side. David remembered that the Lord delivered him before and He could deliver him now. This was in the Old Testament. We have a better covenant in the New Testament. According to Hebrews 13:8 "Jesus Christ is the same, yesterday, today and forever." And, as John 10: 10 says, "The thief cometh to steal, kill, and destroy; I have come that they may have life and have it more abundantly." God has only the best in store for us.

1 Sam 17:45 reads, "...I come to thee in the name of the Lord of hosts, the God of the armies of Israel, whom thou hast defied."

We too have the Name of Jesus Christ. We can slay the Goliath's in our lives with the Name of Jesus Christ of Nazareth. What is the Goliath in your life? God is greater than anything we face.

As our church continues to grow we feel we need sound equipment to have a ministry of excellence. We do not believe God wants us to go into debt for this equipment. We've prayed and we believe we can ask God for the monies we need for this. We are prepared to take a step of faith and pledge R1,000. We're believing God will provide us with R1,000 within the next two weeks to keep this pledge.

After we finished preaching, Betty and I laid our pledge for R1,000 on the altar and then began to sing praises to God. Soon, other people came forward and laid slips of paper on the altar. After the service, we collected the pledges and found that they amounted to R28,000. We were really amazed at the goodness of God. Most of our fifty member congregation made only R400-R500 per month. We rejoiced in the faith of these people and we prayed for them daily.

The following week, I was in Bloemfontein when I saw my friend, Nico. He gave me an envelope that, to my surprise, contained a check for one thousand rands. Out of the blue, Toyota had given me this check because I had purchased so many cars for the L.E.C. Church in Lesotho and this check was in appreciation for bringing Nico so much business. I had always sent many of my customers from the garage to the Toyota dealer to buy their own cars. God had once again provided for us wonderfully and miraculously–

here was money for our pledge. We knew He would do the same for everyone in our congregation. Our people had wonderful testimonies to share with us as well. The money we needed all came in within two weeks. God is so good to us and He loves it when we trust Him.

One lady gave her testimony. She felt led to pledge her rent money and the money had not come to her by the end of the second week. She decided to take a step of faith and gave her rent money to keep her pledge and prayed, 'Lord I will need that money for my rent by Friday.' On Wednesday the Landlord came to the lady and said, "We will be doing some renovations and because of the noise and inconvenience, you do not need to pay rent this month." We were praising God with her for His goodness to us all.

Another Sunday, I was preaching on the name of Jesus and the power in His name. The next day, a visibly shaken young lady from the church came to see us. She related the following story:

> I was on my way home from school today. I kept thinking about the sermon that I had heard on Sunday. I found myself saying the Name of Jesus softly as I rode the taxi on my way home. I never realized that there was so much power in the name of Jesus. I kept quoting the scriptures in Philippians, that 'at the name of Jesus, every knee should bow, of things in heaven, and things in earth, and things under the earth; and that every tongue should confess Jesus Christ as Lord, to the Glory of God the Father.
>
> The taxi let me off a few blocks from home. It was just before noon. The day was sunny and bright. The weather was warm and nice. I felt the presence of the Lord was so real in my life. I felt like Jesus was there with me in a tangible way.

Just as I walked past a clump of bushes, a strong arm went around my neck and roughly pulled me back into the bushes. A man was holding a knife up for me to see, and then pressed it to my neck. He said, "Give me all of your money, or I will kill you." I was really scared. I had no money to give him. I felt so helpless. At that moment, the scripture I had been meditating on rose up within me and I said, "In the Name of Jesus, you will not harm me."

Suddenly he let go. I turned and faced him. He shook uncontrollably and looked at me as if he were seeing a ghost. He dropped his knife. I just looked at him and said softly, "Jesus." He quickly picked up his knife and ran away.

I stood there, still trembling. I decided instead of going home, I would come straight to you and share what God has done.

Betty made her a cup of tea and we continued to praise the Lord together for His goodness in our lives. On the following Sunday she shared her testimony with the congregation.

In this way, our new little church grew. But at the same time, political complications and unrest increased throughout Lesotho–especially in Maseru.

Then I realized. These were not Lesotho tanks. They had been passing our house about every half hour. They seemed to be patrolling. I was beginning to believe that these were South African Army here to help us.

Strangely enough, this gave me boldness to move forward in my escape.

Chapter 37

MORE THAN ENOUGH

Tomorrow, we would get on the plane to return to Africa. Would I have the courage to go, even if I didn't hear from Charles? What would I be returning to? Would we even have a church to go back to? Was Maseru Prep School burned down? I had so many questions that were frighteningly unanswerable I must not think of this any more.

I thought of our church members and prayed that they would be safe throughout this ordeal. Surely God would defend and protect them, as well as Charles. These were people of faith.

As I prayed, I meditated on God's continual goodness in our lives.

As our church grew, so did our praise and worship. At first, I led the praise and worship by myself just using a guitar or a keyboard. Little by little, we added another guitar player, then a bass player, then more singers until finally, we had a real band, except for a drummer. So we made do without.

We began holding mid-week Bible studies in Thaba 'Nchu, a location halfway between Maseru and Bloemfontein.

There were perhaps 100,000 inhabitants in that area when we began our Bible study.

One of our members was Peter Karabo. Peter was a music teacher in one of the high schools in Thaba 'Nchu. Due to some budget cutbacks he was laid off for over a year and at that time he was completely unemployed. During those times, Charles and I would meet with him and his wife, and pray with them.

Eventually, Peter filed a grievance with the school and took another job. When his grievance was finally settled, he received all of his back pay, in addition to being re-instated in his job.

Since Thaba 'Nchu was halfway between Maseru and Bloemfontein, Peter began to attend the church in Bloemfontein on Sundays. However, he would come and visit us occasionally.

One day, shortly after he had received his back pay, he came to see us again. He asked us, "Did you ever get a set of drums?"

Charles replied, "No, we never did, but we will in God's timing."

"Well, I'm going to buy you a set of drums. You meet me at Van Winkle music store in Bloemfontein at two o'clock next Thursday, and make sure to take the seats out of your van."

The following Thursday we went to the music store. We arrived about fifteen minutes earlier than agreed upon. The music store was located in a district populated by lots of second-hand stores. Since it had lots of used equipment, we assumed that Peter would purchase us a used drum set. It would be fine for our purposes. We just needed a set, and someone to play.

We examined the used sets trying to guess which one Peter would buy for us. We eventually picked out the set we wanted. Finally he arrived.

"Have you been waiting for me long?" he asked.

"No," replied Charles, "we just got here a few minutes ago."

"Come, I want to show you the drum set."

As we hesitated at the one we wanted, he walked right past to a new, burgundy-colored set with everything that we needed. It had a bass, snare, tom-toms, several cymbals, and various other percussion instruments. It cost about R2,000.

With a smile and a wave he said, "Here it is! How do you like it? Is there anything else you need?"

Flabbergasted at his generosity, we shook our heads.

Then he turned to the shopkeeper and said, "Load it in their car."

After thanking Peter profusely and praising God continually, we returned to Maseru and to our church with our beautiful new drum set. Now, only one problem remained: who would play it? Charles had played the drums in high school, but it would not be practical for him to play drums and preach. Once again, we simply prayed and asked God to provide the right drummer.

Not too many weeks later, Charles saw a young white lady with two small daughters standing outside the church before services. One of the girls looked to be about eight years old and he guessed the other was about five. Charles approached her and asked, "Won't you come in?"

"Well, I was listening from outside to see if I wanted to come in."

"Well, you are more than welcome."

With that, Charles turned and walked back in for services. Within a few minutes, the lady came in and joined us. The next week we noticed she was in the congregation again, so we made an effort to welcome her. The members of our congregation were also very outgoing, so they tried to make her feel at ease, just as they did for anyone else who came for the first time. Charles would always say, "You are only a stranger one time at this church. After that you are a friend. If you don't feel that way, come see me, because something is wrong."

The lady, we found, was from Denmark. She continued to come to our church and eventually her husband started coming with her. We visited Yetta and Nils several times in their home and enjoyed getting to know them better. They admitted to us that they really wondered if we were for real, but they felt our love for them to be sincere. We watched with amazement at how quickly God was doing a mighty work in their lives.

When we had them over for dinner one evening, Nils noticed our drum set and asked if he could try them out. We were impressed with the way he played. He had all the sensitivity needed to be a good church drummer. Before they left that evening he asked if he could come over and play sometime. We assured them both that they were more than welcome.

As it turned out, Nils came over about once a week to play the drums at our home. His wife called us one day and told us that he used to play in a reggae band. She added that Nils hadn't been a very happy or positive person, but she was seeing a great change taking place in his life. In Nils' past experience with Christians, they had seemed to him to be very phony and he was not keen to become involved in anything having to do with them.

During Nils' weekly visits, he and Charles often talked together. We discovered that Nils' negative attitude resulted from his work. He dealt constantly with the government and the accompanying corruption. Finally one night, Charles and Nils prayed together and Nils became a believer. The transformation that took place in him within only weeks was phenomenal. He became deeply committed to his faith and to the church, and he began to play drums for our services with total sensitivity and submission. What a blessed addition he was!

Nils also volunteered to teach one of our young people, who was very interested in drums, how to play. Every Sunday both of them would lug that set of drums to the church and set them up. Then at the end of the service, they would lug them back to our home where all of the equipment was kept. Michael was an eager learner and he practiced diligently to be ready to play whenever Nils' term in Lesotho was finished.

I thought; our Church is really blessed with wonderful people. I thank God for each and every one of them.

The ringing telephone startled me. As I jumped to answer it, I prayed, "Lord, please let it be Charles."

"Hello!" said Charles.

Chapter 38

CHALLENGES

" Honey, I have good news. Other armies have come into the country and are patrolling the residential areas. They have been passing our house about every half hour. I will leave here at daybreak tomorrow. I am certain that will be an opportune time to try to escape. I will call you the minute I get to South Africa. Bye for now, love you lots."

Betty was relieved to hear that my plan was set into motion. Too excited to sleep, I went to the garage to remove the plates from our car. My biggest challenge would be getting from the house to the border. God help me!

As I struggled with the license plates in the darkness, I focused on God's goodness and found my mind wondering to the many times God helped us.

We were far away from home when our daughter became sick just shortly after we arrived here in Lesotho. The doctors here had no idea how to treat her and we could not go into South Africa; we had to stay in Lesotho. It was then that we cried out to God as our only hope, and what did He do? He touched her little body and healed her completely.

We took our son to the dentist for a check up and the man broke a needle off in the roof of his mouth. We cried out to God and He said, "I AM MORE THAN ENOUGH, TRUST ME!" We prayed daily for our teeth and gums as we brushed them. We never had another cavity the whole time we were in Lesotho and South Africa.

It is evident to me that God brought us together for a purpose. From the night that the people of the First Baptist Church in Chester, by a narrow margin, decided to throw out tradition and allow African-Americans to worship side by side with European Americans, to the time that we first became attracted to each other, to our marriage and throughout our lives, God's hand was always there.

We both wanted to serve God from an early age. It was God who led us to Canada where we could grow as a family without prejudice or persecution. He overcame improbable circumstances to allow us to come to Lesotho and serve Him here. We had learned the hard way that God is our source in every area. We often had to repent of looking to the ways of man (Psalms 118:8) instead of seeing that God is bigger than anything we've had to face. We had called on Him so many times and our answer was there every time.

When those mortar bombs dropped all around us, we called out to God and He protected us.

From my own experience, I knew that if GOD SAID IT IN HIS WORD, then it was true. That gave us more confidence in laying hands on the sick and reaching out to the lost.

This faith was not always easy. Barry took Tina on his bike one day and Tina was barefoot. Her big toe got caught in the wheel and was barely hanging onto her foot. We packed her foot and toe in ice, wrapped a bath towel around it and rushed to the hospital; praying all the way. Blood continued to gush from the wound. The doctor took one look and said, "We'll have to try to sew the toe back on." While he was preparing, we gathered around her, held hands and boldly asked God to heal her completely. (James 5:15) The doctor came back and said, "I don't believe it! This toe is healing already, it looks great! Stay off the foot for two or three days and you will be fine." We took her home and she was running around playing within three days.

We really learned to trust God and He always provided, even when things looked impossible.

We were invited to a pastor's conference in South Africa and we had no visa. We called the visa people and spoke to them about our desire to attend this conference. They explained to us that it would take at least four weeks to obtain a temporary visa for us. The conference was in two weeks. We asked them to really try and they said they would do what they could but would not promise anything.

We prepared to attend the conference and kept speaking the Word of God over our visa. We declared that our visa would be at the border according to Job 22:28. Many people kept asking us, "Has your visa come yet?" We always replied, "It will be at the border waiting for us."

The time for the conference came and we drove to the border. I got out of the car and handed the man at the window our passports.

"You do not have a visa and you cannot enter South Africa."

I replied, "My visa was faxed to the border, please check your records."

He came back quickly and shoved our passports towards me and said, "There is no visa here for you."

I felt a holy boldness come upon me and I said, "Please check again, I know our visa is here"

After almost ten minutes, he returned, with a temporary visa for us and we attended the conference.

MORE CHALLENGES

One day we went into town to go to the bank. We had just parked our car. It was hot and dry and our car windows were open. Before we could get out a big army land rover pulled up beside us. An army officer began to get out and he was holding an automatic rifle of some kind. The car was higher than he realized and as he got out he fell towards our car and his rifle hit me in the side of the head. He felt bad and apologized and Betty and I just praised God that I was not hurt; just a little sore.

Another day Betty was driving into Maseru from Morija and I had warned her on numerous occasions to be very careful and concentrate on her driving. She shared with me that she was busy praising the Lord and praying when all of a sudden, it was like an audible voice in her car that said "SLOW DOWN!" She said it was so real she wondered how anyone could be in her car, but she slowed down immediately. Then she noticed at the crest of the hill there were two taxi's (Kombi type) coming straight for her. If she had not slowed down she would have been hit head on. She said she drove much slower the rest of the trip and concentrated on her driving. We were both praising God again for His constant protection.

When we lived on the farm one Thursday evening we were all going to church and we decided to take two cars. Betty and I left first and Tina and Barry were behind us. We were going about 50 k per hour (about 35 mph) when we crested a slight hill and found the road full of sheep. I slowed right down and stopped until the road was clear enough that we could go on. Betty said, "I pray the kids will see those sheep and have time to slow down." The kids later related their story to us.

Tina was driving. They both had seat belts on. They could see the dust from our car ahead of them. They came over the crest of the hill and were shocked to see the road full of sheep. Tina hit the brakes and screamed. The car skidded. Barry yelled, "Get off the brakes!" Barry grabbed the steering wheel and tried to steer into the skid. Tina quickly let go of the steering wheel and put her hands on her face.

The car took off into a field, missing a huge rock only by inches. (About two months previously a young man was killed in his car at about that same spot when his car hit that huge rock head on. Again, the road had been full of sheep). The car began to roll over and over until it came to a halt and landed on its roof. When the car stopped, both Barry and Tina were hanging upside down, held only by their seat belts. They walked away from that accident with minor cuts and bruises. The car was a total write off. Another lady was right behind them because she too was on her way to church. She stopped and gave them a lift into town. We were shocked to see them come into church covered in dirt, little cuts and looking really shook up. We praised God and rejoiced in His mercy.

Only about two weeks before we were leaving Lesotho/ South Africa to return to the United States; we were coming home from Ladybrand into Lesotho. It was dark and traffic was heavy. We were in the Venture. The Venture was made by Toyota and was similar to a truck but would hold eight passengers. It was very handy to us in the ministry. We used it to haul our equipment when the seats were down and to transport people when the seats were up. It had a bulbar on the front. Betty had just said to me, "Look at all this traffic." All of a sudden it was right in front of us. A black half gown calf. He turned and seemed to be looking straight into my eyes. We both saw it at the same time. I could not miss it. I tried to steer a bit to the right but there was traffic coming right at me. We hit it. It was like hitting a wall. THUD! The cow swung around and hit the door on Betty's side of the car. Our windscreen was splattered with blood and debris. I couldn't believe we were still moving. We slowed down and pulled off the road a little further down. The Venture was so damaged, we could not open the door on Betty's side. The cow was dead.

We have always known that we must never be out at night, on the highway. No one stopped to help us; we knew we would have to try to go on. We decided to drive the car to the border of Lesotho. We limped back onto the highway and drove slowly all the way to the border. Our headlights were of very little use to us. They no longer showed on the highway, they were shining up into the sky. We reported the accident and limped home. For the next two days the car was being repaired and we were praising God for His angels, that obviously, we were keeping very busy.

I knew it was now or never. Time to go. It was just before dawn. It was very quiet. It seemed like nothing was moving. The shooting, which was sporadic, continued in the distance. The smoke was still thick and hovering in the sky. I looked around quickly and saw no one. I listened, but heard no tanks, or movement of any kind.

I carefully and quickly opened our gate, drove through, locked it behind me, and cautiously, but swiftly headed for the border.

I drove cautiously, constantly looking around me. I saw burned cars and rock barricades all around with huge amounts of debris everywhere, frequently forcing me to maneuver to keep from puncturing a tire. I saw no other vehicles or even a human being; nothing or no one. The scene was eerily surreal. When I reached the border crossing, it appeared that there was no one at the border at all. The area seemed completely abandoned. I almost panicked.

What should I do now? If I drive through and someone is watching, I could be shot.

I made a split second decision. I accelerated and sped through the border. No shots rang out. I arrived safely at the South African side.

As I showed my passport to the attending officer, I said, "I saw no one at the border. There was no one to check my passport on that side, so I just came through."

"How is it over there? No one has come through here for a couple of days now."

"There is a lot of fire and a lot of fighting still going on, but I've seen tanks patrolling the residential areas." I replied.

"Yeah, I've seen a lot of smoke and I can hear the shots, but no one is using the border these days."

He shook his head and I slowly continued to drive to our friends' house on the farm just before Ladybrand. They were very glad to see that I was safely out of Maseru.

I called Betty. She, Barry and Tina were overjoyed to hear that I had arrived safely in South Africa. They were sure angels had escorted me to the border. We looked forward to meeting in Johannesburg.

I was praising God. We would be together as a family again soon. Praise God!

Chapter 39

DREAMS

The Maseru downtown business district was almost completely destroyed by fire. Charles and I spent the next year bringing food into Lesotho and training the people in the church to see God as their source in every area. Due to the destruction, many people were now without work. We needed to reach out to one another more than ever.

In November of 1999, we attended the annual leaders meeting for Christian Revival Churches in Bloemfontein. At the meeting, all the leaders were asked how long we felt God wanted us to stay in our churches. In other words, what was everyone's vision for the future? After talking and praying about it, Charles and I felt that God was leading us to stay at least another five years. We felt by then there would be more leaders raised up and the church would be much more stable. We committed to serve for five more years in the church in Maseru. And, we also signed a five-year lease for the house in which we were living.

On January 19, 2000, I had a strange dream. In it, Charles and I had gone to Bloemfontein to have a meeting with Pastor At. During the meeting he looked straight at us and said, "Charles, we're going to replace you in Maseru because it is time for you to return to America." As the dream continued, Charles agreed with him. I could not believe it, "This cannot be true. We just agreed to stay here for another five years. God is not a God of confusion, how can this be happening?"

The next day, we were reading our Bible together, using Max Lucado's Inspirational Bible. We came across the scripture in Genesis 30:25-26: "Now let me go to my own home and country. You know that I have served you well."

I continued reading the life lesson for that day's readings. The inspiration section said: 'He knows what we are doing, what we are learning, and how He is going to use all of that five, ten, twenty years from now. When the signals are blurred and you are uncertain, keep on praying, getting Christian counsel, but don't stop what you are doing.'

I kept reading further: 'God knows how to move you when the time comes for you to be moved. He knows what is happening to you, and what should be happening to you. In other words, trust God to be God. There isn't anything He doesn't know.'

As I told Charles about my dream, he answered, "Betty, I know now that God is speaking to us. I too had a very similar dream last night. In my dream, we went to that meeting in Bloemfontein, and I said to Pastor At that I knew we were to return to the United States."

I stared at him in unbelief, unwilling to accept the meaning of these dreams.

Charles knew what I was thinking. He tried to comfort me, "Now, Betty, don't worry about it. He did not say we must pack up and leave right now. God will confirm His Word. We will do nothing and say nothing until God confirms that this is what He really wants. We will continue running the race that the Lord has set before us."

After that I put it out of my mind completely. I refused to give it a thought until I knew without a doubt that this was of God.

On April 11, I came upon this verse in Genesis 31, verse 3: "...return to the land of your fathers and your kindred and I will be with you."

I just stopped and looked at those words. I mentioned it to Charles. It was then that he told me that God had been speaking to him, too.

In our daily readings together that day, the Life Lesson Inspiration read: "Changes are in the air right now. It's disrupting, isn't it? I need you to go out on a limb and move. Take your family and move overseas. I have a special work for you. It's time for someone else to take charge."

On April 12, our devotions took us to Exodus 23, verse 20: "I am sending an angel ahead of you, who will protect you as you travel. He will lead you to the place I have prepared."

"Let's call Pastor At and schedule a meeting with him next week," Charles said. "We must share this with him."

We knew we could not leave the flock without a leader. Charles kept assuring me that we were not leaving just yet. God would work out everything.

We had our meeting with Pastor At the following week and Charles began to tell him why we had come.

"I already know," he interrupted. "God has revealed to me that you will be returning to the United States."

Astounded, our faces must have shown our surprise. He already knew!

From there, we had to discuss the timetable. We had scheduled another home leave in June. I thought maybe we should not go at this time. Pastor At insisted we go as planned. He was sure God would speak to us further and we would know the date we had to leave. Everyone agreed to meet again in mid-July. Charles and I also decided to say nothing to anyone until we knew exactly when we would be returning to America to stay.

Chapter 40

CLEAR PATH

W hen we walked out of that meeting, our two major concerns were selling our cars and selling our furniture.

On our way back to Maseru, we stopped in Ladybrand. A friend walked up to Charles and offered him the exact price we had just been talking about and hoping to get for our car. Charles accepted the offer. The car was sold and paid for that very week.

God was showing us again that when a person is ready to obey Him and to do all He asks, He will bless him in abundance for "He doeth all things well, and very well indeed."

Later that evening, we got a telephone call from another friend of ours from Johannesburg. She asked, "Betty, do you know of anyone in Maseru who is leaving and wants to sell some furniture? My folks have bought a big farmhouse and they don't have enough furniture for such a big house."

I paused, not knowing what to say. Charles and I had agreed to tell no one that we were leaving. I asked her to hold and spoke to Charles about it. He thought this was of God and I should share with her. I hesitantly explained to her that we might be leaving, but we were not saying anything to anyone at this time.

"Well, your secret is safe with me. I won't tell anyone. Why don't you fax me a list of everything you want to sell and what you want for it? I can send you the money now and wait to move the furniture out after you've gone. How does that sound?"

God was working out every detail.

That lady bought almost everything we had and transferred the money into our bank account within a few days.

As we prepared for home leave in June, it dawned on me that we had signed a lease for the house. To break it would require six month's notice. It was already May. We decided to speak to our landlady.

The next day we drove to Ladybrand to visit her. She greeted us and said, "Before you say anything, I want you to know that I know you will be leaving Lesotho."

Both Charles and I were speechless.

"Don't look so shocked," she continued. "I will say nothing until after you do. And don't worry about the lease agreement, the house, or anything. I know you will do what God leads you to do."

We just nodded, in awe, of the hand of God in our lives.

"What about your furniture?" she asked.

"Most of it is already sold to a friend of ours. There were a few things left that we forgot to list."

"Please don't worry about selling the rest of it. When your furniture goes, if there is anything left, I'll buy the rest of it–all of it. You just make a list of the things that remain and what you feel they are worth. I will buy it all."

We could not believe our ears. God did not leave out a single detail. He had taken care of everything.

We kept our meeting with Pastor At in the middle of July. We still had heard nothing definite on a date. When Pastor

At asked about it, Charles suddenly replied, "I feel God is saying the end of August or the first of September."

"That's exactly what the Lord has said to me–the end of August."

"Wow!" I thought to myself, "That's only six weeks away."

On our way home I asked Charles, "When did you get the dates?"

"Just as he asked me."

Again, every detail was worked out for us.

It took us exactly three weeks to pack up our personal items and send them on ahead to the United States. While packing, I realized that there were many little things that I did not know what to do with. Then, Charles and I developed the idea to set those things out in the garage and invite the congregation to come and help themselves to anything they wanted.

Chapter 41

NEW REVELATION

W e wondered about selling our van. It was only two years old and worth a lot of money. Who would buy it? Charles decided to call the Toyota dealer and speak to Nico about it. He said to Charles, "Man, just bring it to me when you are ready to leave and I will buy it from you." Charles told him how much he wanted and he agreed the price was right. Everything was going so well!

Above all, I was very concerned about the people of the church. As I prayed and read God's Word for comfort and direction, the reading from The Inspiration Life Lesson in Joshua read: "Leaders don't lead forever, even godly leaders. There comes a time in every ministry when God calls for a new beginning."

It went on, "There was continuity from one leader to the next, but there wasn't always conformity, for each leader is different and must maintain his or her individuality. A wise leader doesn't abandon the past but builds on it and he or she moves towards the future."

Wow! Now I was getting excited. God was constantly reassuring me. Every question I had, He was there to comfort, lead, guide, and direct and He was always ready to provide in every way. He continually moved things out of the way for us and made our work so easy. We simply trusted Him in every area. He proved to be more than enough, always!

The reality of our departure from Lesotho was not easy for either of us–especially for Charles. I usually expressed my thoughts and feelings easily. Charles pondered his thoughts and spoke to God alone. He knew that telling the congregation about our leaving would be difficult. We decided to call a leaders' meeting and tell the leaders first. We also decided to write out what we wanted to say, just in case it was a bit emotional; it would be easier to read a statement.

We began the meeting with praise and worship. Charles stood up to speak about how important it is to obey God, when one of the young men at the back of the room began to cry. As he continued to speak, more people began to cry. Everyone had solemn looks on their faces.

He said to them, "The Lord called us to plant this work in Maseru and God told us that we had accomplished that. I kept wondering why we must leave at this time, but then God reminded me that some plant, others water, but he brings the increase."

When Charles looked up and saw almost everyone crying, he was unable to speak further. Suddenly, one of the young ladies rose and walked to the front. She read the rest of the notes that Charles had prepared and opened the meeting for discussion.

Many in the group had already known. Charles reassured them that he was sure that this was God's will, and that there would be very good leaders to take over the work of the church. We would not leave the congregation stranded. At the end of the meeting Charles encouraged them to continue with the vision and to work harder than ever to bring many into the kingdom of God.

On the following Sunday, Charles and I both shared with the congregation how the Lord had led us to this point, sharing with the church the Word that God had given to us. We shared how God had moved every mountain for us. We assured them that they were ready for new leadership and that God would give them the right leadership. Of course everyone wanted to know who it would be, but Charles and I did not know at that time. We closed the service by saying everyone was welcome to come by our home and take whatever little thing was left there that we were not taking with us. We had laid everything out on pieces of cardboard on the garage floor.

Almost everyone walked over after church and within minutes everything was gone. They all seemed so happy to be able to keep something of ours as their own. I was very happy that God had given us that idea.

Chapter 42

FAREWELLS

W e felt sad when we realized that there were only two more Sundays left before we would leave Africa. During the following week, many people called us and assured us that this was of God. The deacons came to inform us that we would only preach one more Sunday. On our last Sunday, we were invited to come as guests. They had asked another preacher to come and give the message.

On that final Friday, the truck came for the furniture that was to go to our friends. That was a difficult time for us both. It made the decision so final. Charles held my hand as I wept.

The landlady came to buy the things that were left in the house. I gave her the list and prayed that we had made the right decision on the prices.

She took the list and gave us an envelope, saying, "Now don't argue. I know God wants me to do this."

We thanked her as she left. When we opened the envelope, we found that she had given us much more than we had asked.

We walked out of our practically empty home for the last time and drove our van to the dealer in South Africa who had offered to buy it from us. Again God gave us favor. Nico gave us more money than we had asked. God was continually blessing us!

That night we were invited to stay at a guesthouse in Ladybrand. The landlady and the pastor and his wife from the church in Ladybrand asked us to dinner. It was a nice, quiet, relaxing time together. The following night, they asked Charles and me out again, but this time we were met by a number of members from our previous church in Ladybrand for a surprise farewell party. Everyone had a really good time of fellowship.

As we looked around at each face around about us, we knew we would miss these beautiful wonderful people whom we had grown to love so very much. When we returned to our room, we thanked God for His goodness and asked him to take sadness away from us.

We went back to Maseru for our last night and stayed with our best friends, the deacons. They took us to church the next day. The church leadership had planned a beautiful farewell for us, including lunch. The young people did a hilarious skit impersonating both of us. The choir sang a song that one of the members had written about us. One of the young men did a rap, which was especially touching to us. Many got up to make speeches about us.

After a huge delicious lunch, gifts, hugs and tears, the church presented us with a video of the occasion. By four o'clock in the afternoon, our deacons drove us to Bloemfontein. We arrived at our mother church just before the evening service. In the middle of the service, the senior pastor called us up and prophesied over us.

After the service, all the pastors went to the VIP room for food and fellowship. We bade our deacons and very good friends good-bye before they left for Maseru.

Pastor Nyretta and Pastor At spoke and presented us with beautiful matching watches. Pastor At said to Charles, "Charles, as your last official act as a pastor in our church,

I want you and Betty to pray and lay hands on all of the pastors in this room–including me–that your anointing of 'Pastor' will be upon all of us."

After the service, we were privileged to stay with one of our best friends, Pastor Charles, and his family. We had stayed with them often when they were in the area and we loved this family very much. That was another difficult goodbye.

The next day we all had a braii (South African for barbeque) with all of the pastors and their families in a local park. We had a lovely time and there were no tears.

Early on Tuesday morning, we boarded a plane and headed home to the U.S. We were happy to hear that the right leaders stepped into the roll as pastors in Maseru and the transition went very well–only two weeks after our leaving. God is good, all the time!

Chapter 43

FULL CIRCLE

O ur family met us at O'Hare airport in Chicago and our
son took us into his home to live with him. We knew
we were to be in the United States, but we were not yet sure
where we would live and how we would serve our Lord.
We spent several weeks just relaxing and praising God for
His continued goodness to us. We found a church with an
excellent pastor and wonderful teachings. Within a few more
weeks, we began to serve in this church in the prayer center.

One day, we got a call from Pastor Ron Coleman asking
us to speak in his church in Chester, Illinois (our home town).
Charles was more than happy to do this. While in Chester,
Charles decided to see our local doctor. At that point, Charles
disclosed to me that he had been experiencing some discomfort in his chest when he did certain things.

The doctor examined him and decided to send him to
Missouri Baptist Hospital in St. Louis for further tests. I
wanted Charles to get back to the Chicago area and see a
doctor there. Our doctor in Chester said, "No, you must not
put this off. We'll just do it now." We called our kids and told
them we would stay in this area a bit longer and have these

tests. They decided to come and be with us, even though Charles insisted it was not necessary.

The next morning after Charles had his testing, the doctor called us into his office and showed us that the main artery to Charles' heart was 99% blocked. The doctor said that they rarely see this kind of blockage. Usually the patient has a massive heart attack and is gone. They call it the 'widow maker'. The doctor said the hospital would try to get a team ready to do the operation NOW. He advised us that Charles may not even live through the weekend without this surgery.

I was stunned! Was this why the Lord brought us home so suddenly? We both had a physical in South Africa about six months before and they said we were strong and healthy. I called Pastor At in Bloemfontein, South Africa, and asked him and the pastors there to pray for Charles with us. We prayed with Charles and they rolled him into surgery. We waited and prayed and interceded for over six hours. It seemed like years!!!!

Afterwards, the doctor came in and said everything went well; they did a triple bypass. They also said Charles had veins like a young man and they expected his recovery to go well. He would be in intensive care for the next 24 hours or more. We truly rejoiced in the Lord. It was another hour or so before we could see him. He was sleeping nicely. We returned to Chester and went back the next day to find Charles' eyes wide open. He was glad to see us. His recovery was going very well and the next day they moved him into his room. The staff told us they would give Charles a pill to help him sleep and we should come back tomorrow. We left to return to Chester.

Back in Chester, our friends met us at the door and said, "The hospital called. You must return immediately, Charles had a fall." Barry and I headed right back to Missouri Baptist Hospital. We could not imagine what had happened. I tried not to think about it, I just prayed all the way.

When we got there, we found that Charles had had a bad reaction to the drugs they gave him. He had hallucinated, gotten out of bed (over the rails) and pulled a tube out of the main artery to his heart.

Apparently, that set off all the bells at the nurse's station. They found him quickly and got the tube re-inserted before he bled to death. Charles suffered terrible hallucinations the rest of the night.

Praise God, the hospital staff decided not to give him any more drugs. His recovery proceeded without further incident.

We had much to praise God for. We enjoyed our time with our children and especially with our granddaughter. The longer we stayed in the Chicago area, serving in the church and sharing lots of loving memories with our children, the more we felt a pull towards Chester. Charles had a mother, two brothers and a sister in Chester and we would go that way about four or five times a year. Every time we were there we always visited Grace Church Ministries and usually tried to have some fellowship time with Pastors Ron and Connie. We just felt so much at home at Grace Church. Upon our return to the Chicago area, we kept wondering if we were where God wanted us to be.

We began to seek God and His will for us more diligently. We certainly did not want to push any doors open, but we continually yearned to serve Pastors Ron and Connie. We cried out to God and turned it over to Him. We learned many years ago that He always has a perfect plan that never fails.

One Sunday while we were in Chester, we went out to lunch with Pastors Ron and Connie. Pastor Ron said, "When are you guys ready to move to Chester?" He went on to explain that they had felt for some time the need for Care Pastors to minister to the shut-in's and the folks at the nursing homes. Man! We were excited! We knew this was God.

We started looking for a place to live in Chester. One of the first houses we saw seemed perfect for our needs. It even came with furniture. We had nearly nothing of our own because we had been living with our kids. The house we wanted was for sale and we wanted to rent, so we kept looking. After many weeks and seeing nothing that we wanted, we went back to that first house and negotiated to buy it. We agreed upon a price and went to the bank, wondering if we could get a mortgage. Within three weeks, we had purchased the house and moved our few personal items into our new home. This house even contained linens, dishes, spices and canned goods for us. Again, our loving Father had proven Himself strong on our behalf.

As we settled into our new home and in our new job, I kept praising God for His goodness to us. Sometimes, it is difficult to comprehend that we are back where we started so many years ago. I ran into a former high school classmate and she said to me, "Betty, I'm so glad you left Chester when you did, I was actually afraid you would be killed." Then she proceeded to tell me that one night (during that period of gossip) there were chalk outlines all around the post office of killings. The sheriff had to get the fire department to scrub down and clean the sidewalks.

We were in a local store one day and a lady said, "Did you just move into that house that was for sale?" When we said "yes" she proceeded to say, "I live just a few doors down and I wanted to welcome you to the neighborhood. It's so good to have you as neighbors." We chatted for a few moments and continued shopping. I'm constantly amazed at God's power and His timing in bringing us full circle, back to Chester; bringing us home to serve Him here.

Chapter 44

AFRICAN VISIT

O ur returning to South Africa in February 2007 was not at all what we expected. I guess we really never know how many lives we touch – how different things would be had we not been there or said that word or served God there at that time.

Many years ago Charles finally took that step of courage to tell me how very much he loved me and my spirit leapt because I knew I too was in love with him. At that time we had no idea what ripples, what storms, what adventures, what blessings, would come to us because of our love for each other. Neither did we have any idea how our lives together would touch and change so many other lives all the way across the world.

I remember well that I used to cry out to God many times. I kept asking: Why did we fall so deeply in love when we could never be married – in Chester, Illinois? I was so naïve. Everyone seemed to know that I was in love with Charles long before I knew it. I actually thought EVERYONE loved Charles. We did not even know we had done something 'wrong' when Charles gave me a lift to church one evening. We were only friends. The very next morning I started getting nasty obscene threatening phone calls. I could not figure out what was happening. It got a lot worse before it got better. My Father told me that some people even wanted to run Charles and his family out of town. For what? What had we done? How could we ever hope to get married?

It seemed like everyone was against us, except for our families; and they too worried about our safety and prayed for us a lot, wondering if we should not choose to take separate roads. I did not plan to fall in love with Charles. I always dreamed of getting married some day, having a big wedding and a beautiful white wedding dress. We never really courted. If and when we saw each other, it was often in fear, wondering if we were being watched.

Matthew 19:26b...with God all things are possible. All we could do was wait and trust God. God never fails. God faithfully showed Charles we could live in Canada. It was hard to believe how different things were in Canada. It was like a different world. We could go anywhere, eat in any restaurant, stay at any hotel, ride any bus, go to any movie – it was wonderful. We had such a good time together. We lived in a basically white world – but no one seemed to notice we were different.

Later God led us to Lesotho (Southern Africa) where we lived in a black world and EVERYONE noticed us. Again I wondered why South Africa? Years previously God told me I would marry a Pastor and I would serve in Africa; but I never thought we would go to South Africa during Apartheid (racial segregation). It was even against the law for us to travel in our car together as a married couple; or as a family. I didn't see it at the time, but God had a plan and we got a little bitty glimpse of His plan while we were in South Africa this year. We're still awe-struck! It's hard to fathom. We really had no idea! God had a perfect plan from the very beginning.

We were speaking to Pastor At Boshoff on our skype phone one day and he insisted that we must come for a visit, so we agreed that we would come in February the following year. That trip was amazing.

We were blessed to be able to attend many of the church services at CRC in Bloemfontein while we were there. We also attended staff meetings and leaders meetings. Our first Sunday in church, Pastor Nyretta Boshoff introduced us as one of the first pastors that worked with them in Ladybrand when they started out in the ministry. As I recall there were about 20-25 people meeting in a hall in those days. Pastor At Boshoff again introduced us in the evening service. He even called us up on stage and said, "This couple worked with us, supported us, stood with us, almost from the very beginning of our ministry." Then he looked us right in the eyes and said, "I want to say to you, in front of all these witnesses (over 7,000 people in that service) that because you believed in me, this work is where it is today." Everyone cheered and clapped. We did not expect him to say anything like that. We had dinner and fellowship together after the service.

At another service, one of the pastors we had worked with came and sat beside us and said, "Look over at that section of people over there." As we looked, he said, "All of those people. They are here because of you; because you were here. You can see your work, right in front of you." We did not know what to say but Praise the Lord!

A few days later we had lunch together with Pastors At and Nyretta. Then they shared with us that it was because we always believed in them and saw God's call upon their lives and this has kept them going and serving. Their church is now over 17,000 people and they expect it will be 25,000 by the end of this year. Pastor At insisted that they wanted to bless us while we were there and they would take us where ever we wanted to go. They put us in a beautiful guest house and provided pastors to care for us. We found that hard to accept. We had gone there to serve, to bless, to preach and to share in the work there during our visit. Pastor At made it very clear that God told him to bless us and he intended to do it. He also took very good care of us. He did not want us to travel a lot because it was so very hot. He said people could come visit us here and that's basically what happened. They made us feel so very special.

Pastor At knew he was called to have an integrated church – during Apartheid – and with Charles and I being leaders in the church, and Pastor Edward coming in as a black pastor in the work, this church was the first in Ladybrand to become integrated. It is still integrated today – and is a church of about 400 in a community of about 5,000. Later when Pastor At moved to Bloemfontein then we became the Pastors of Christian Revial Church in Ladybrand. That in itself was an act of God, because we were still in Apartheid. The people loved us and the church continued to grow.

We were well aware that Charles and I being together was a shock to most of the white South Africans. A few that came to church and saw us there never returned. Most were very pleasant to us and grew to love us, but at first meeting it was not always easy. It never occurred to me how the black South Africans viewed us, until this most recent visit. Pastor Albert (a black Pastor) drove us to Maseru Lesotho and spent the day with us. He shared with us what an honor it was for him to be able to drive us where we wanted to go. Then he proceeded to tell us that meeting us so many years ago made him deal with his thoughts and preconceived idea's. It never occurred to us that the blacks too were dealing with issues they had never been faced with until meeting us. We all had a good time together and went to many places in Lesotho and visited many pastors and friends. Pastor Albert said he was amazed that so many people knew us. He told us that every-where we went people were saying, "Look! They're back! I haven't seen them for years." They were speaking softly in their own language and Pastor Albert heard it all.

It was really good for us to return to Lesotho and South Africa and see the growth in the churches there and see the Pastors and friends that we love so much.

We found ourselves wondering....we had struggled so many years ago, even to get married...and yet mixed churches are growing in leaps and bounds...in South Africa. We saw clearly that God makes the difference.

Another day we spent a whole day in Ladybrand. What a joy to see the people and friends there. Most were not aware that we were coming for a visit and were really surprised to see us. Many of the youth that served faithfully in the church when we were there went on to Bible School and became Pastors of their own churches.

We flew to East London to visit one of the churches there and we spoke at one of their services. We just shared together a simple message of faith and trusting God in every area. That was also an integrated church. We had such a good time of fellowship with them.

More than anything else, while we were in South Africa, we felt the love of Pastors At and Nyretta and the people. Everywhere we went, we felt special, we felt loved. Everyone was so eager to 'serve' us. It was truly awesome.

Proverbs 15:33 The fear of the Lord is the instruction of wisdom; and before honor is humility.

EPILOGUE

It is our prayer that you will see in our book, the power of God, the love of God, the consistency of God, the hand of God and the protection of God.

God cares about everything we care about so much more than we realize.

God continually shows us that He is all we need; He was and still is more than enough.

Phil. 2:13 For it is God which worketh in you both to will and to do of His good pleasure.

When Maseru was burning and I was still there, we cried out to God, and He brought me out safely.

Too many times we let the things around us look too big for God. It is the prayer of our hearts that you will see that God is more than enough. He desires that we live in His perfect peace. We can only do that as we keep praising Him and trusting Him to be big enough in every area.

Our time in Africa stays with us as a memory that we live every day. Each day we pray for our friends and fellow workers in both Lesotho and South Africa. God sent them into our lives to enrich us.

We are learning that His Grace is sufficient for everything that we must do, and His Love is sufficient for everything that we are.

These are just a few of the many stories that made their way home with us from Africa. Hopefully we will have more to share with you in our next writing.

We love you! God loves you even more!

This is the story of our spiritual journey. We share how we met, how the Lord brought us together, and how we were married. In our search for personal freedom, the Lord took us to Canada where we lived for eighteen years and adopted our two children. In 1978, the Lord called us to Lesotho and South Africa, where we served for twenty-three years. Our story is about His direction, His protection and His leading in our lives.

CPSIA information can be obtained at www.ICGtesting.com
Printed in the USA
LVOW061154080413

328004LV00001B/1/P